MONSTER & MADMAN

THE SECRET HISTORY *of* JACK THE RIPPER AND FRANKENSTEIN'S MONSTER

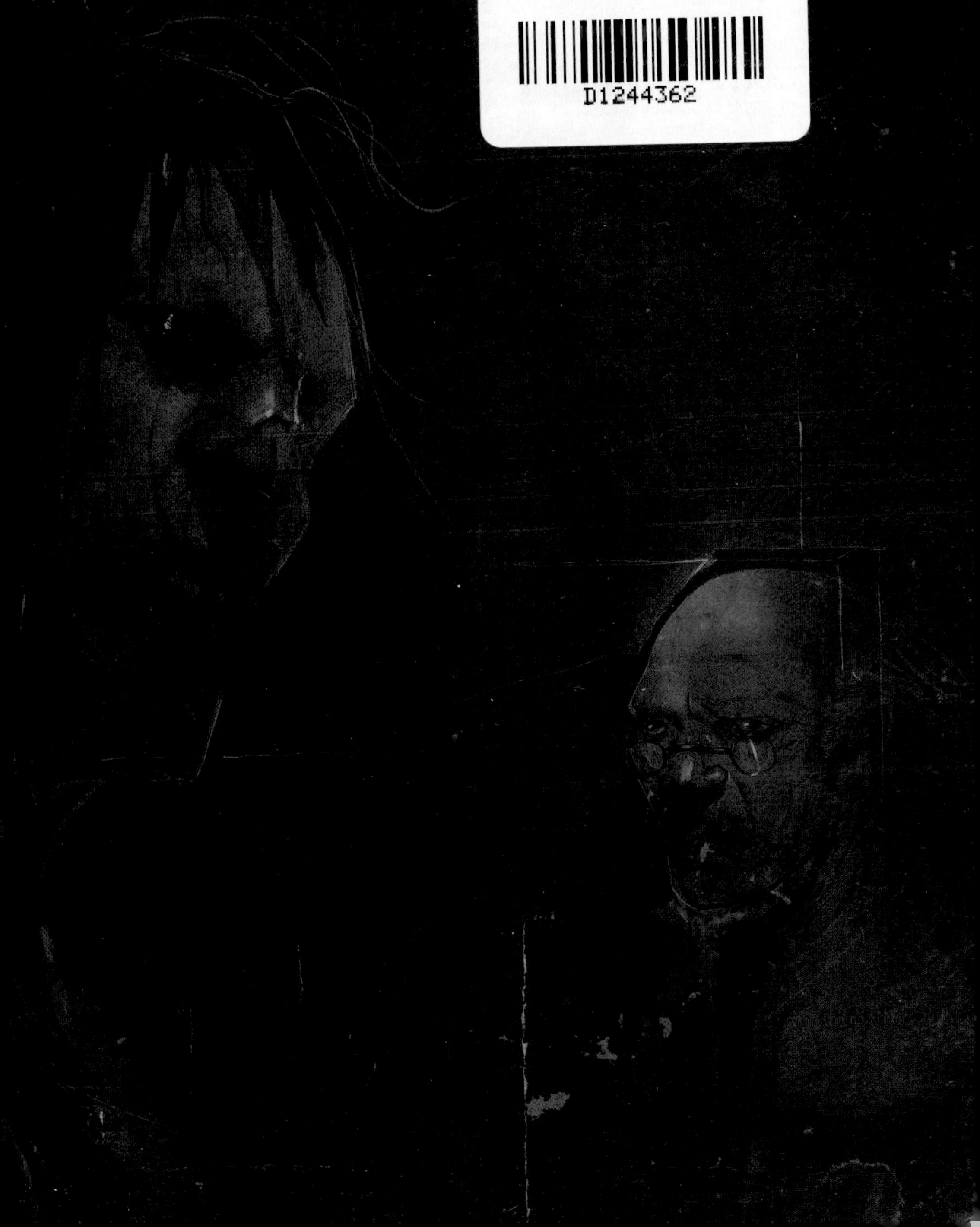

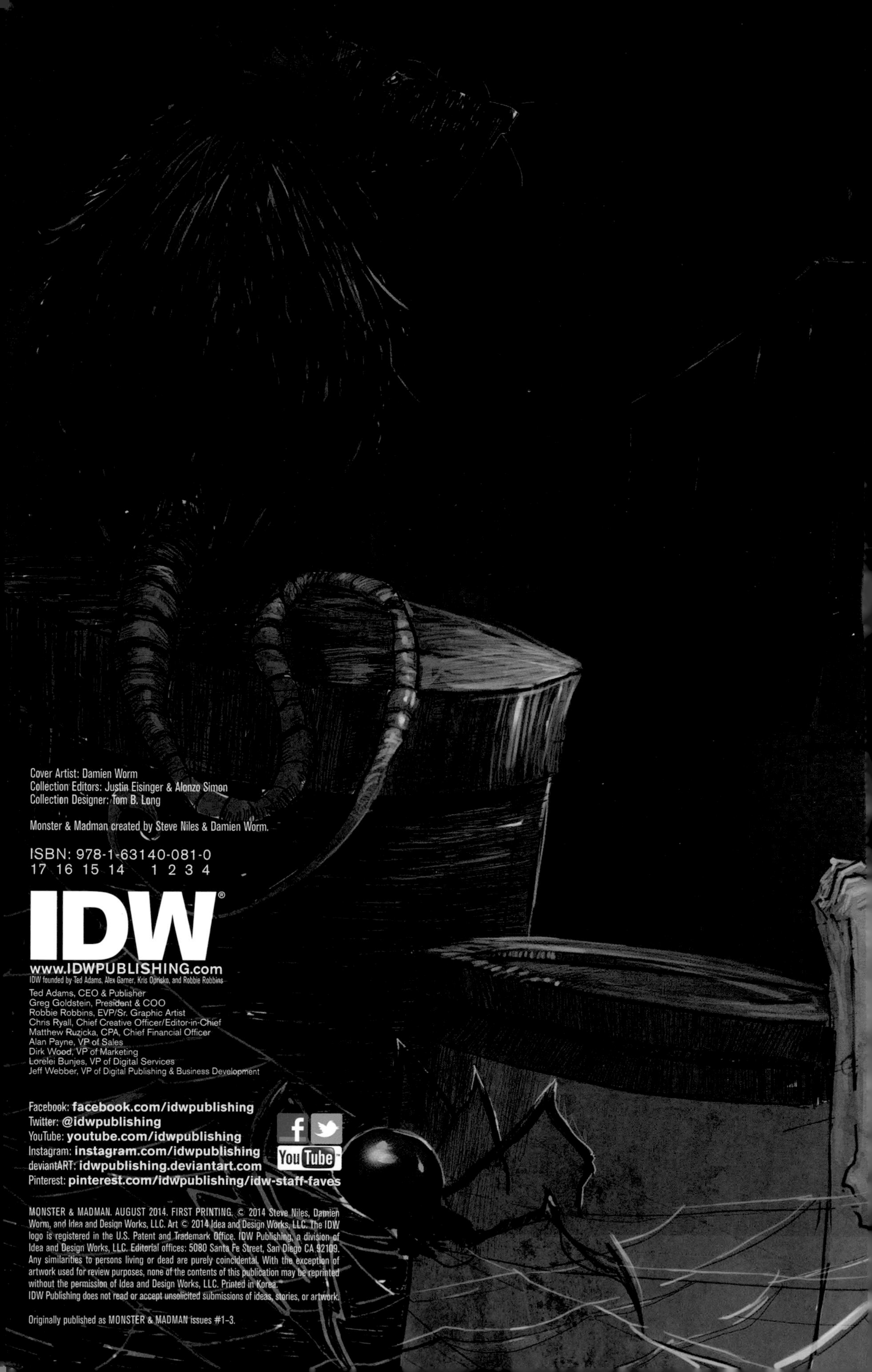

Cover Artist: Damien Worm
Collection Editors: Justin Eisinger & Alonzo Simon
Collection Designer: Tom B. Long

Monster & Madman created by Steve Niles & Damien Worm.

ISBN: 978-1-63140-081-0
17 16 15 14 1 2 3 4

IDW®
www.IDWPUBLISHING.com
IDW founded by Ted Adams, Alex Garner, Kris Oprisko, and Robbie Robbins

Ted Adams, CEO & Publisher
Greg Goldstein, President & COO
Robbie Robbins, EVP/Sr. Graphic Artist
Chris Ryall, Chief Creative Officer/Editor-in-Chief
Matthew Ruzicka, CPA, Chief Financial Officer
Alan Payne, VP of Sales
Dirk Wood, VP of Marketing
Lorelei Bunjes, VP of Digital Services
Jeff Webber, VP of Digital Publishing & Business Development

Facebook: **facebook.com/idwpublishing**
Twitter: **@idwpublishing**
YouTube: **youtube.com/idwpublishing**
Instagram: **instagram.com/idwpublishing**
deviantART: **idwpublishing.deviantart.com**
Pinterest: **pinterest.com/idwpublishing/idw-staff-faves**

Originally published as MONSTER & MADMAN issues #1–3.

MONSTER & MADMAN

THE SECRET HISTORY *of* JACK THE RIPPER AND FRANKENSTEIN'S MONSTER

Writer:
Steve Niles

Artist:
Damien Worm

Series Editor:
Chris Ryall

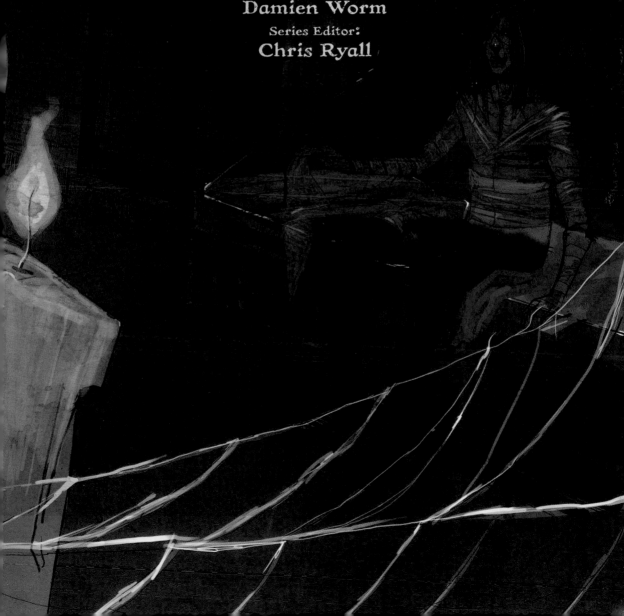

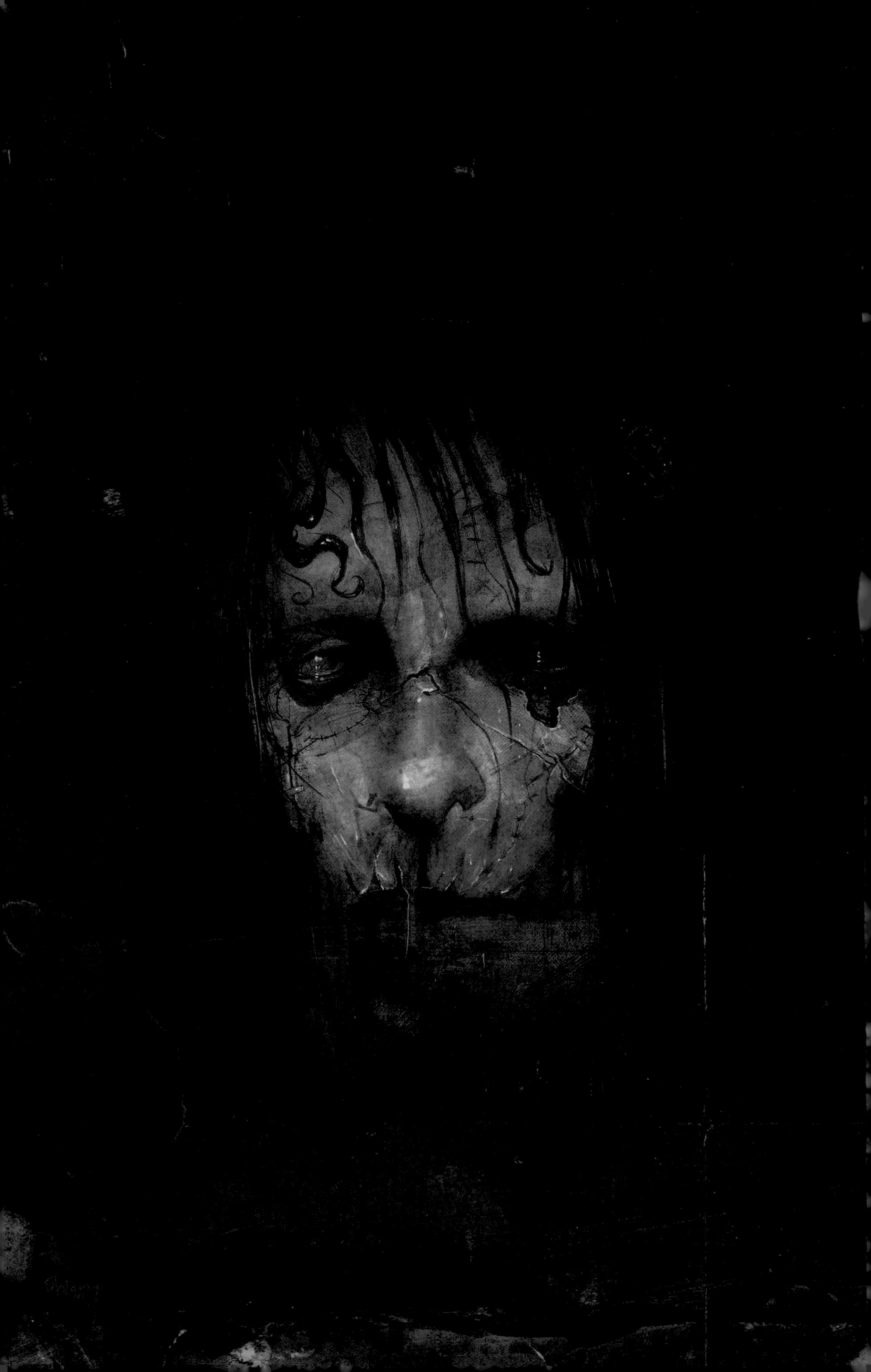

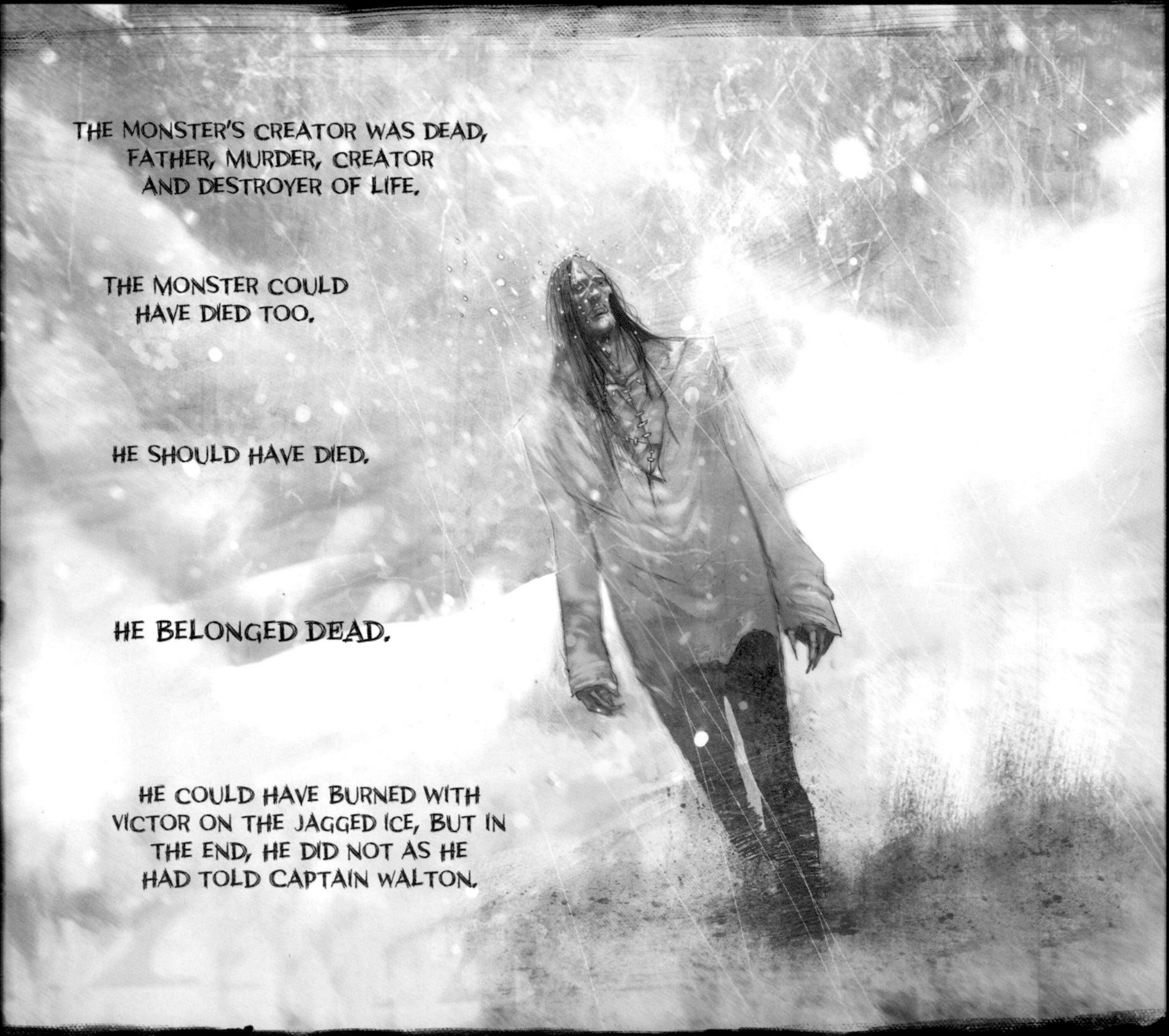
THE MONSTER'S CREATOR WAS DEAD, FATHER, MURDER, CREATOR AND DESTROYER OF LIFE.
THE MONSTER COULD HAVE DIED TOO.
HE SHOULD HAVE DIED.
HE BELONGED DEAD.
HE COULD HAVE BURNED WITH VICTOR ON THE JAGGED ICE, BUT IN THE END, HE DID NOT AS HE HAD TOLD CAPTAIN WALTON.

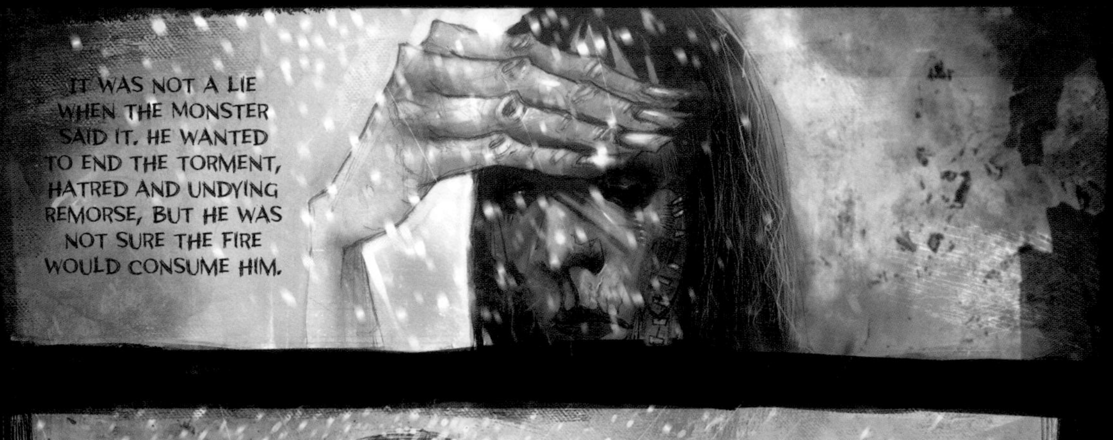
IT WAS NOT A LIE WHEN THE MONSTER SAID IT. HE WANTED TO END THE TORMENT, HATRED AND UNDYING REMORSE, BUT HE WAS NOT SURE THE FIRE WOULD CONSUME HIM.

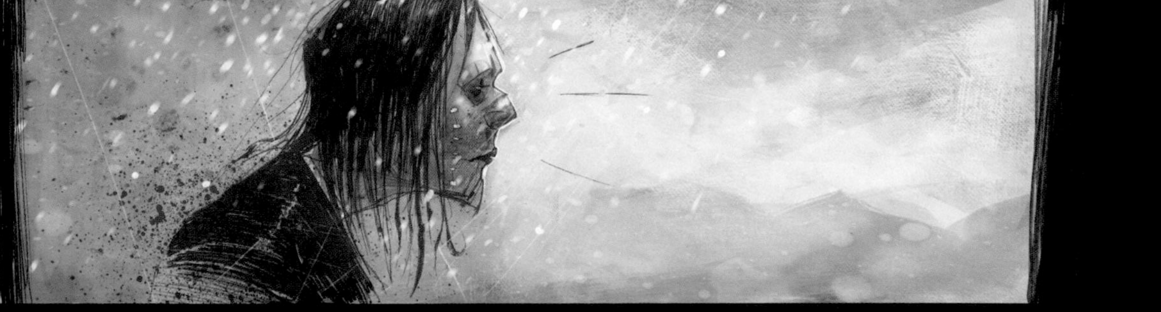

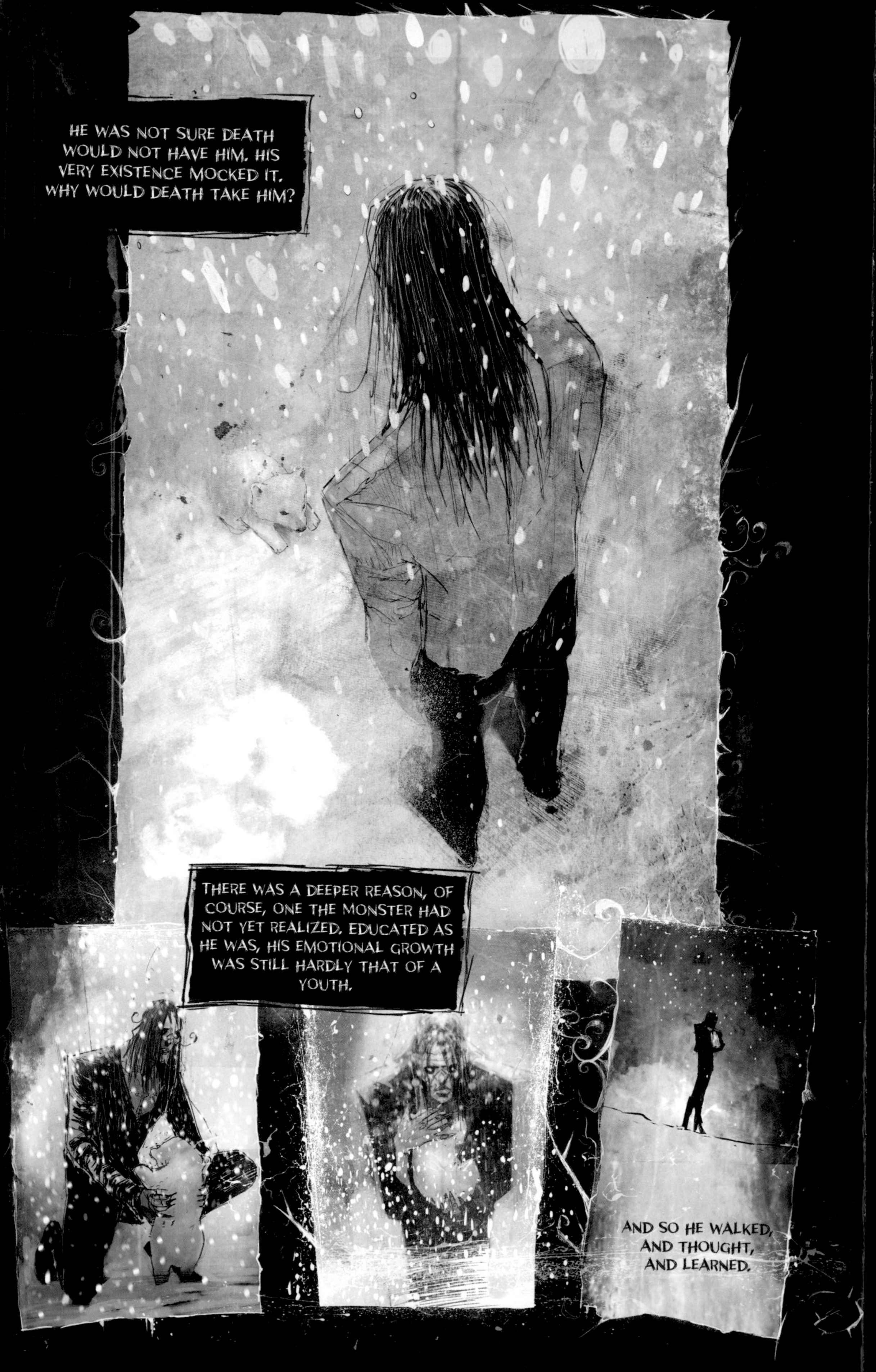
HE WAS NOT SURE DEATH WOULD NOT HAVE HIM. HIS VERY EXISTENCE MOCKED IT. WHY WOULD DEATH TAKE HIM?
THERE WAS A DEEPER REASON, OF COURSE, ONE THE MONSTER HAD NOT YET REALIZED. EDUCATED AS HE WAS, HIS EMOTIONAL GROWTH WAS STILL HARDLY THAT OF A YOUTH.
AND SO HE WALKED, AND THOUGHT, AND LEARNED.

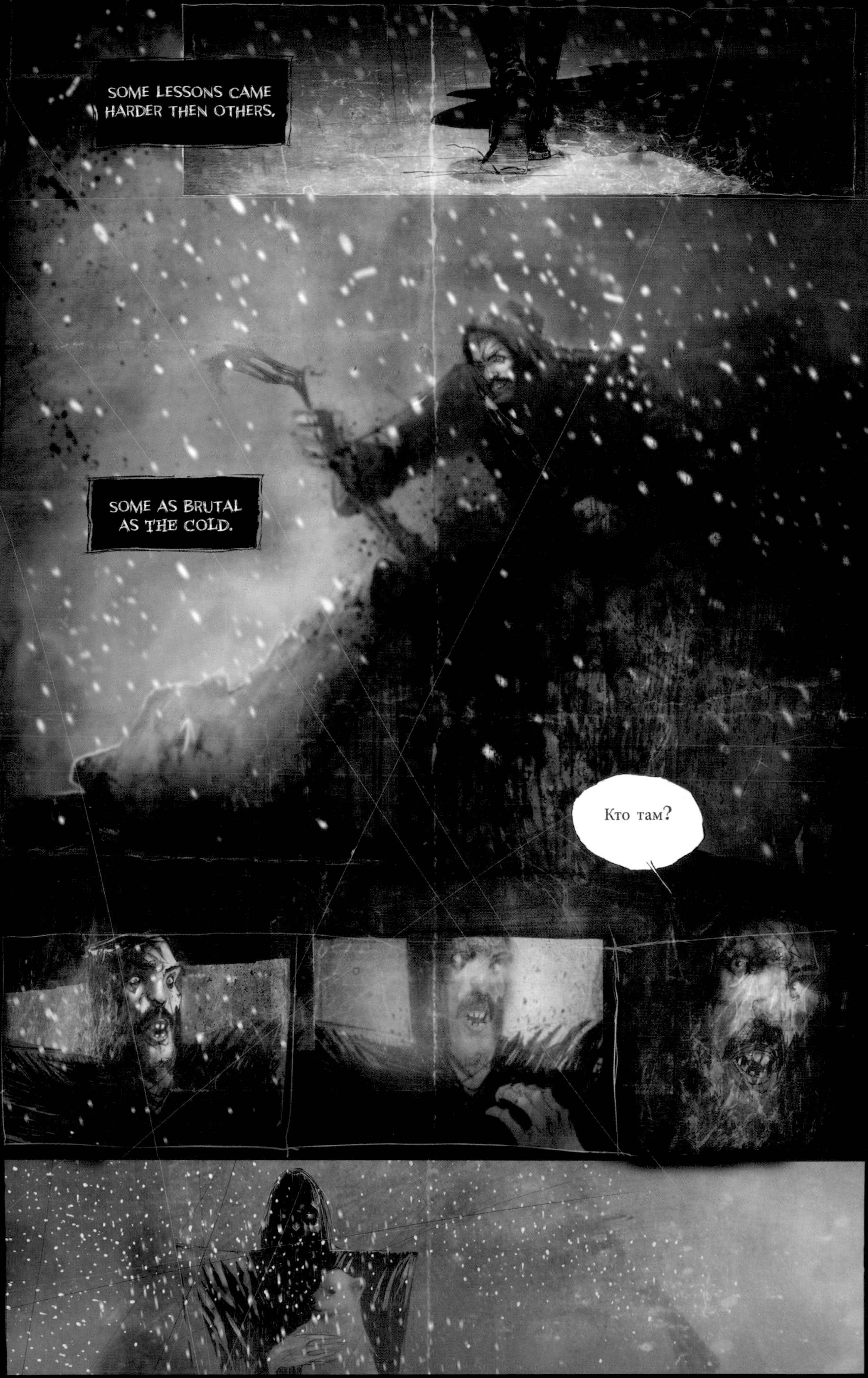
SOME LESSONS CAME HARDER THEN OTHERS.
SOME AS BRUTAL AS THE COLD.
Кто там?

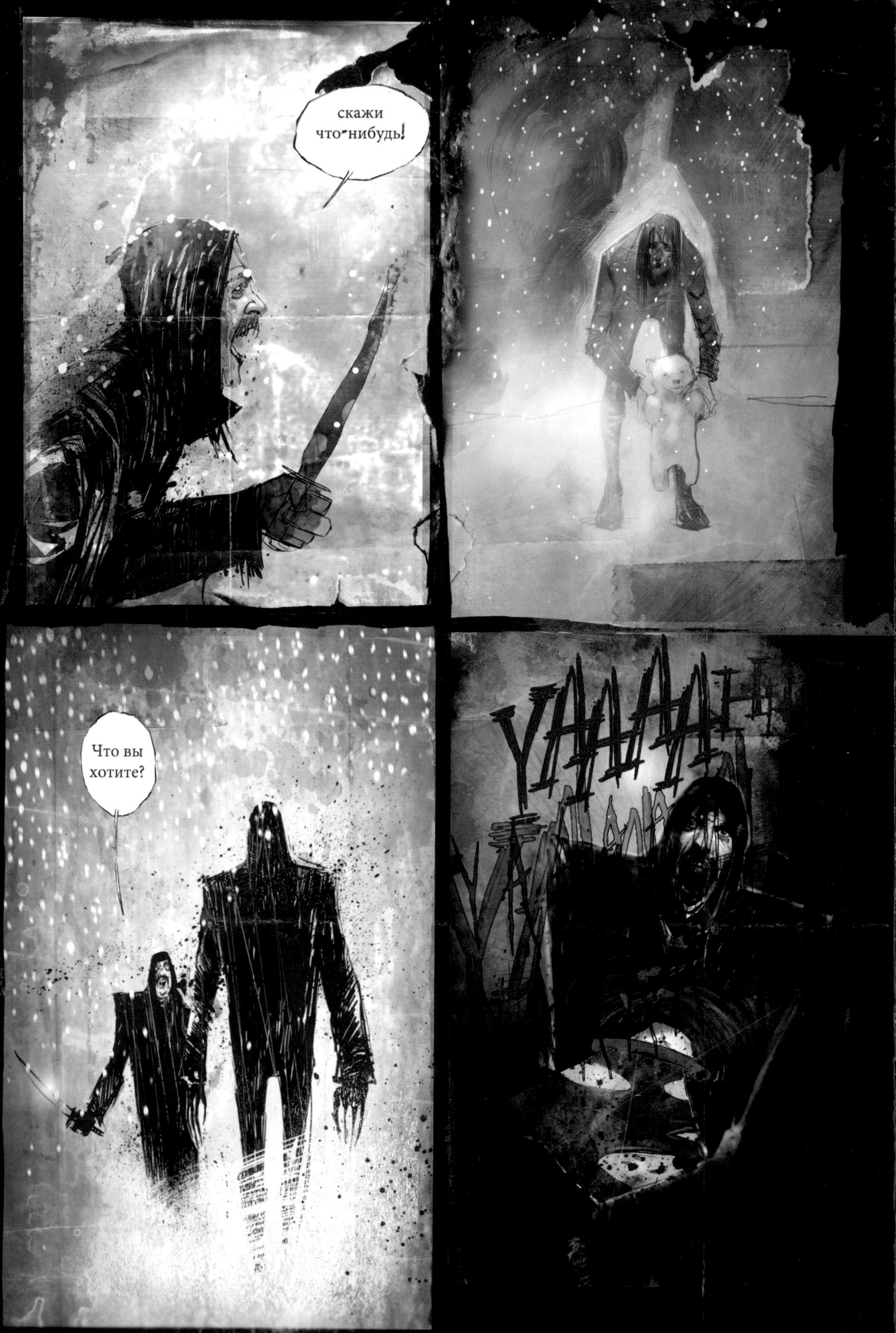
скажи что-нибудь!
Что вы хотите?

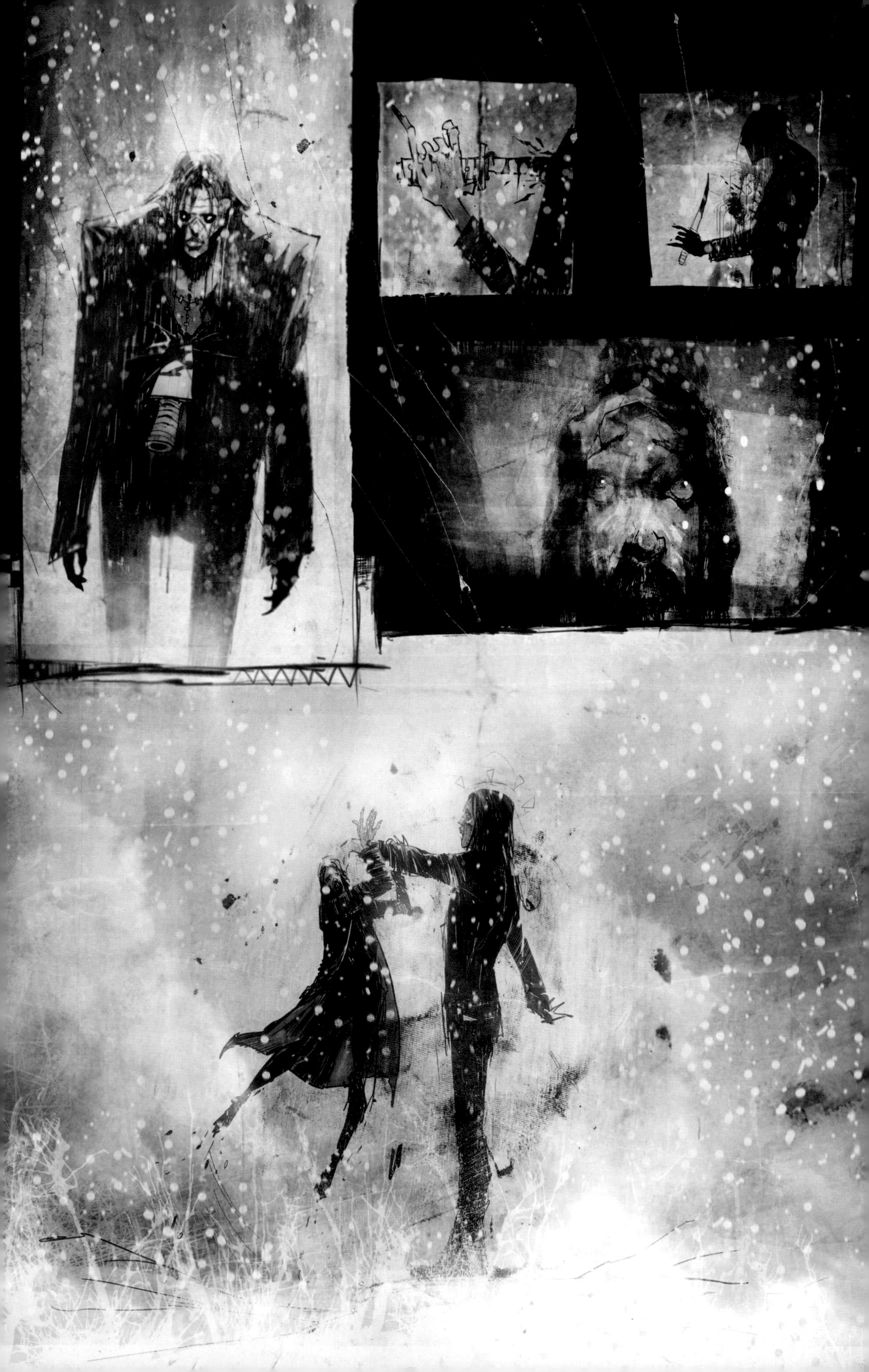

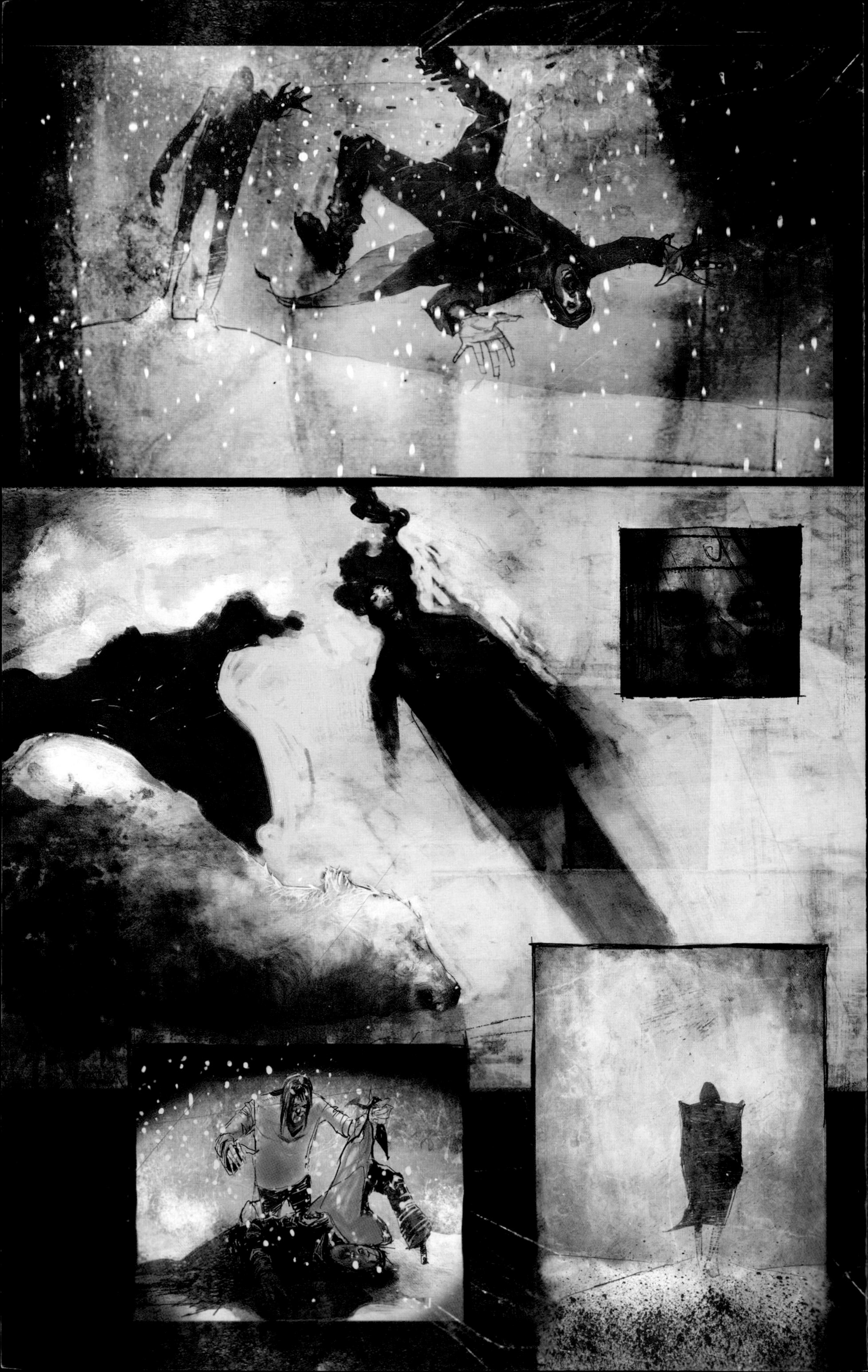

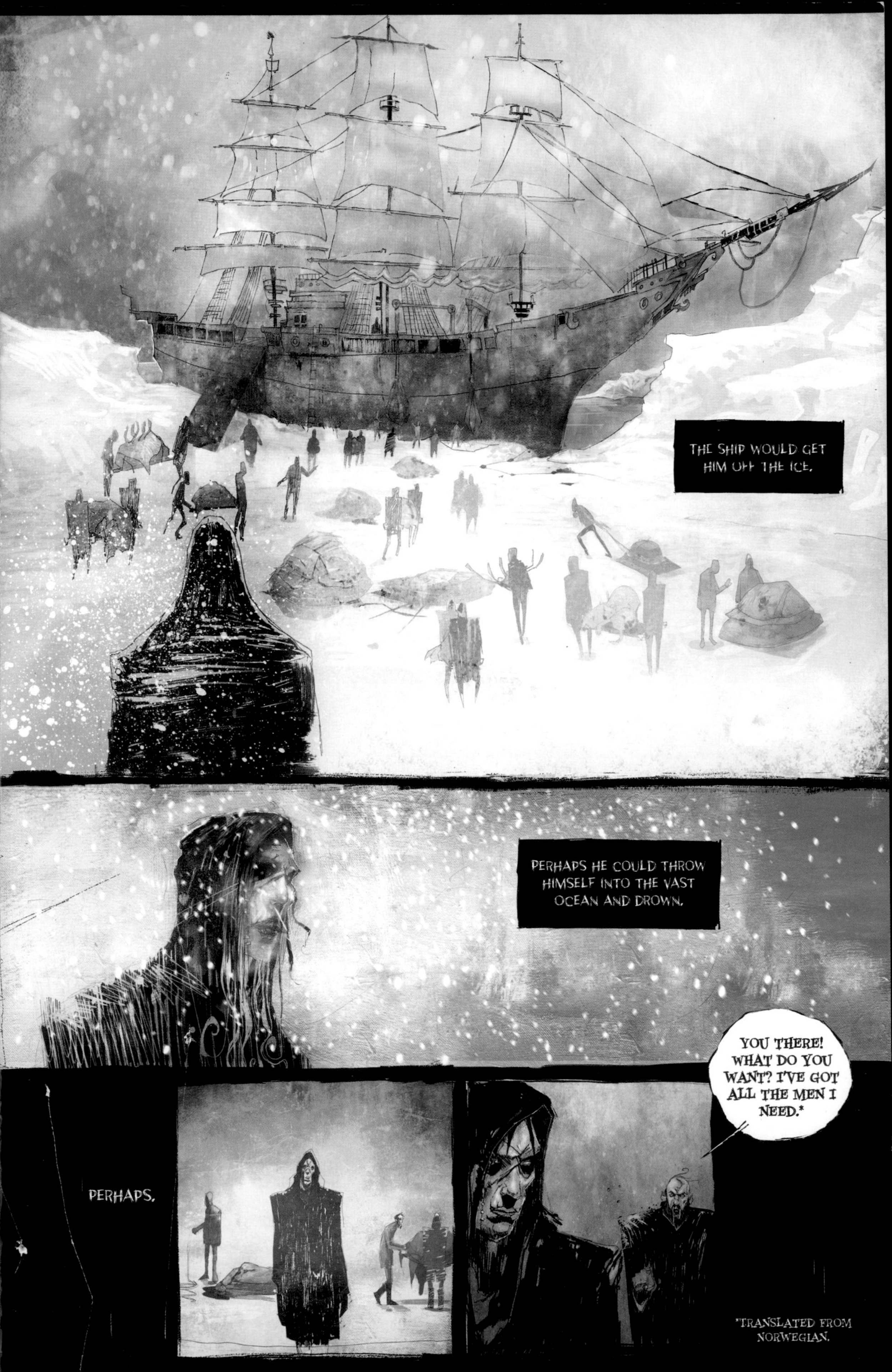
THE SHIP WOULD GET HIM OFF THE ICE.
PERHAPS HE COULD THROW HIMSELF INTO THE VAST OCEAN AND DROWN.
PERHAPS.
YOU THERE! WHAT DO YOU WANT? I'VE GOT ALL THE MEN I NEED.*
*TRANSLATED FROM NORWEGIAN.

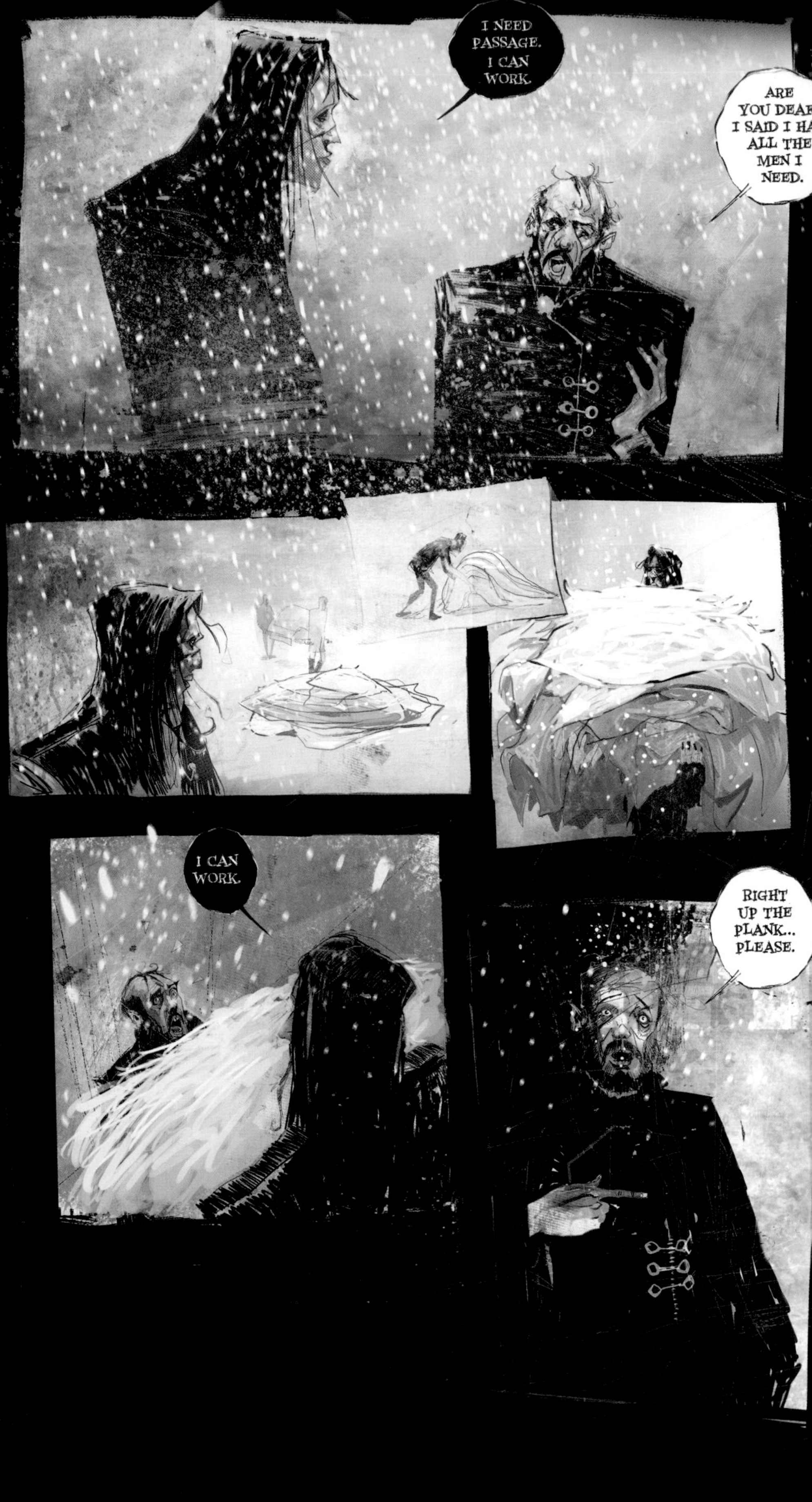
I NEED PASSAGE. I CAN WORK.
ARE YOU DEAF? I SAID I HAD ALL THE MEN I NEED.
I CAN WORK.
RIGHT UP THE PLANK... PLEASE.

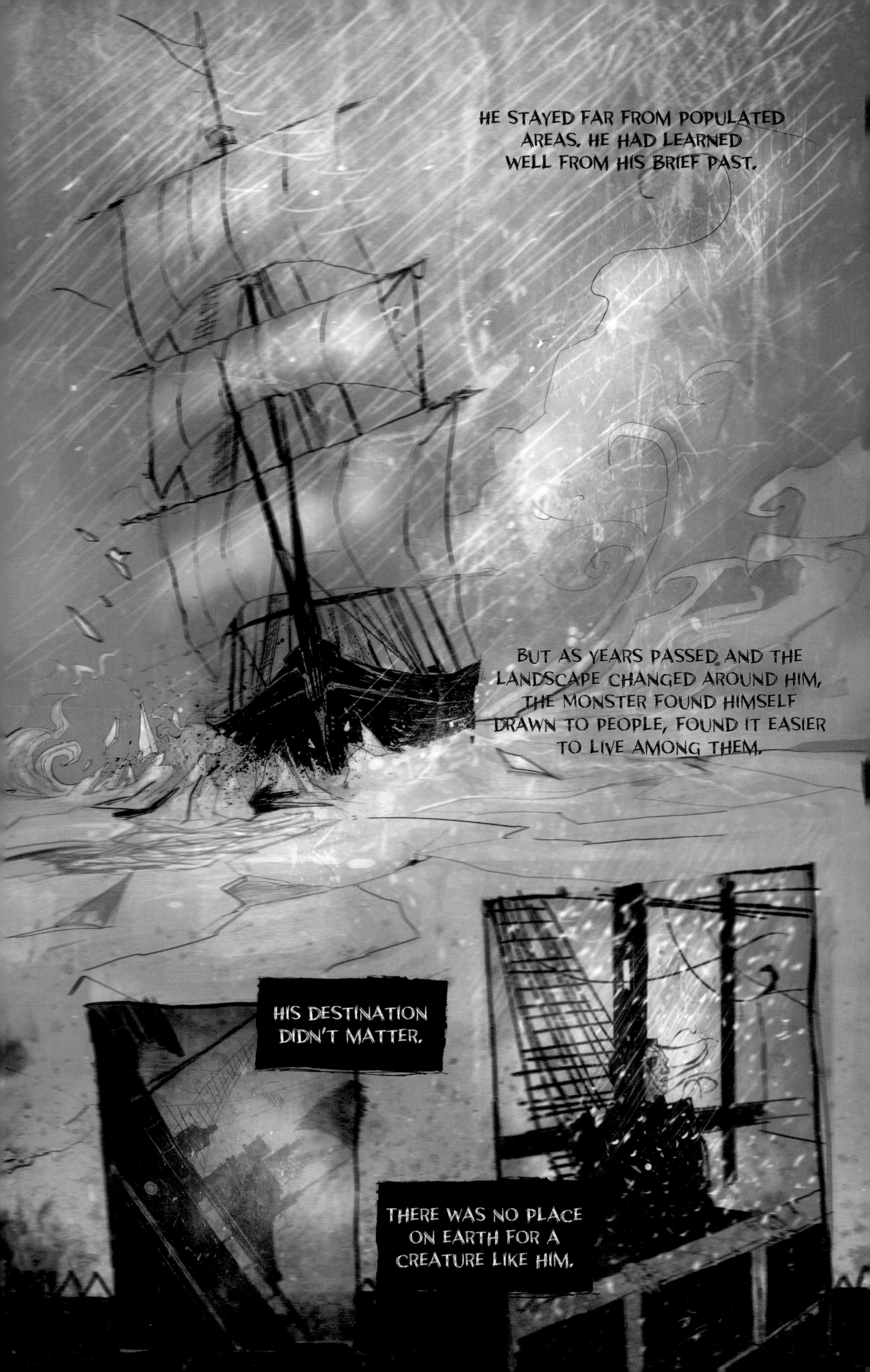
HE STAYED FAR FROM POPULATED AREAS. HE HAD LEARNED WELL FROM HIS BRIEF PAST.
BUT AS YEARS PASSED AND THE LANDSCAPE CHANGED AROUND HIM, THE MONSTER FOUND HIMSELF DRAWN TO PEOPLE, FOUND IT EASIER TO LIVE AMONG THEM.
HIS DESTINATION DIDN'T MATTER.
THERE WAS NO PLACE ON EARTH FOR A CREATURE LIKE HIM.

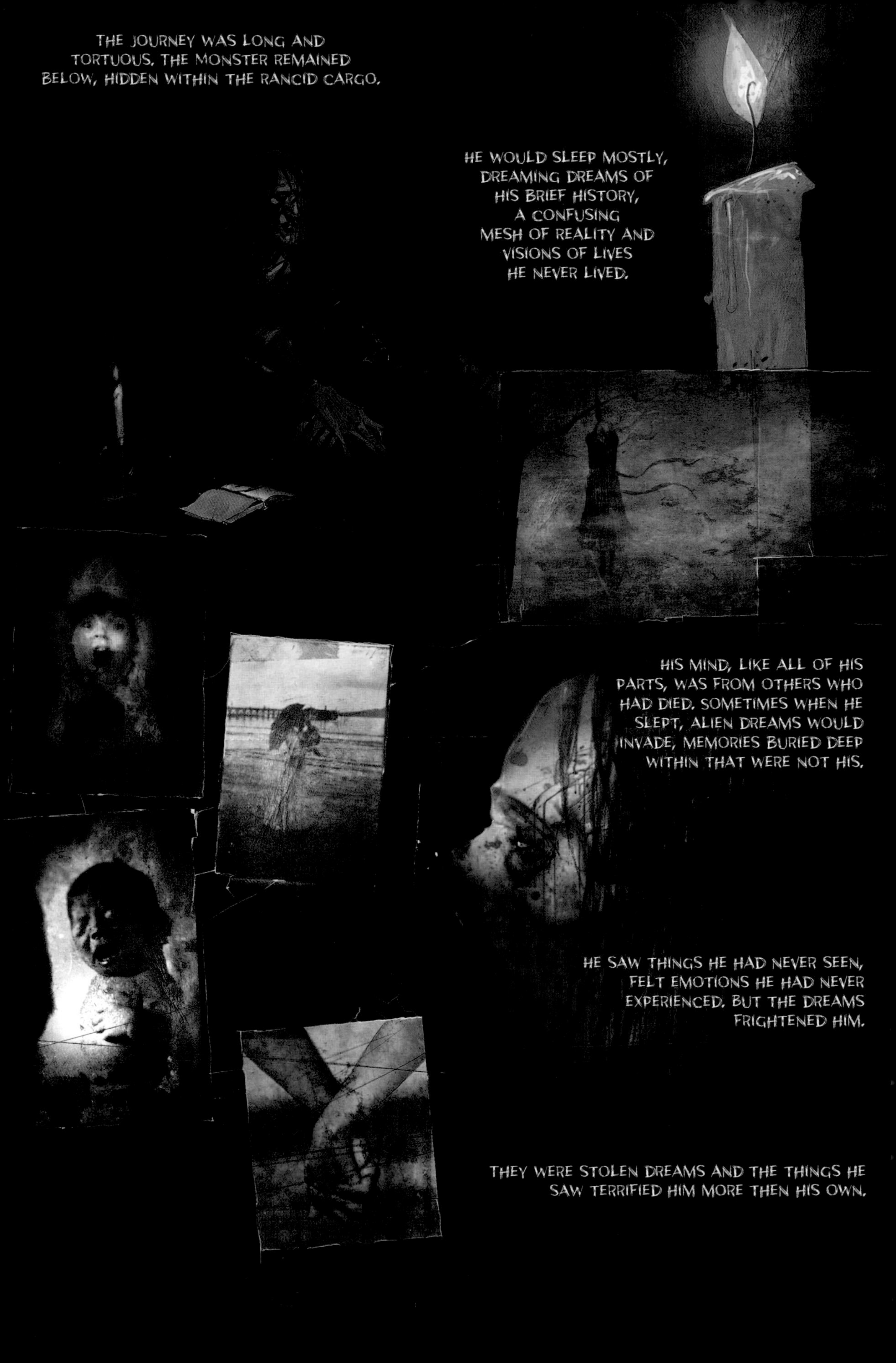
THE JOURNEY WAS LONG AND TORTUOUS. THE MONSTER REMAINED BELOW, HIDDEN WITHIN THE RANCID CARGO.
HE WOULD SLEEP MOSTLY, DREAMING DREAMS OF HIS BRIEF HISTORY, A CONFUSING MESH OF REALITY AND VISIONS OF LIVES HE NEVER LIVED.
HIS MIND, LIKE ALL OF HIS PARTS, WAS FROM OTHERS WHO HAD DIED. SOMETIMES WHEN HE SLEPT, ALIEN DREAMS WOULD INVADE, MEMORIES BURIED DEEP WITHIN THAT WERE NOT HIS.
HE SAW THINGS HE HAD NEVER SEEN, FELT EMOTIONS HE HAD NEVER EXPERIENCED. BUT THE DREAMS FRIGHTENED HIM.
THEY WERE STOLEN DREAMS AND THE THINGS HE SAW TERRIFIED HIM MORE THEN HIS OWN.

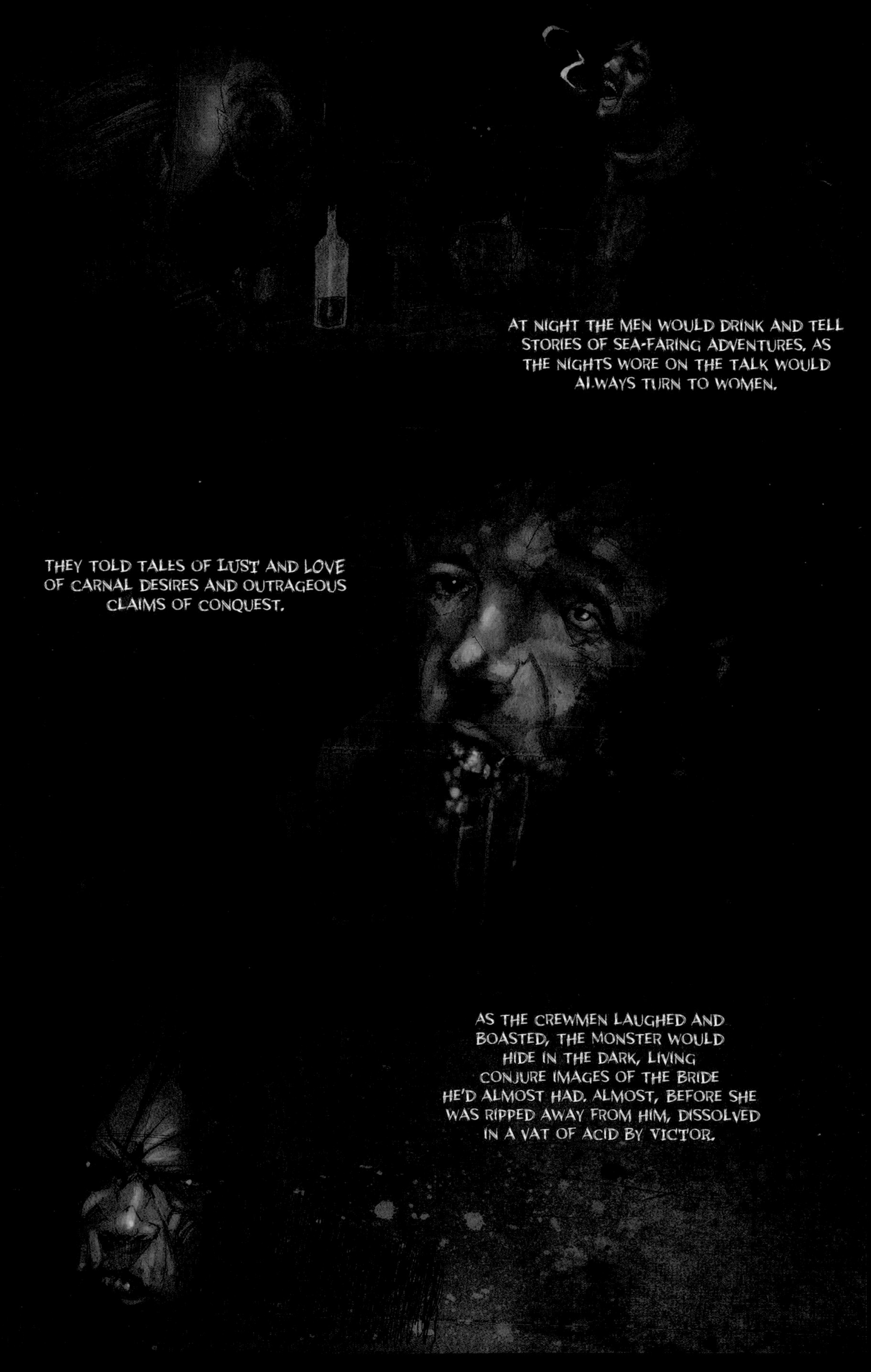
AT NIGHT THE MEN WOULD DRINK AND TELL STORIES OF SEA-FARING ADVENTURES. AS THE NIGHTS WORE ON THE TALK WOULD ALWAYS TURN TO WOMEN.
THEY TOLD TALES OF LUST AND LOVE OF CARNAL DESIRES AND OUTRAGEOUS CLAIMS OF CONQUEST.
AS THE CREWMEN LAUGHED AND BOASTED, THE MONSTER WOULD HIDE IN THE DARK, LIVING CONJURE IMAGES OF THE BRIDE HE'D ALMOST HAD. ALMOST, BEFORE SHE WAS RIPPED AWAY FROM HIM, DISSOLVED IN A VAT OF ACID BY VICTOR.

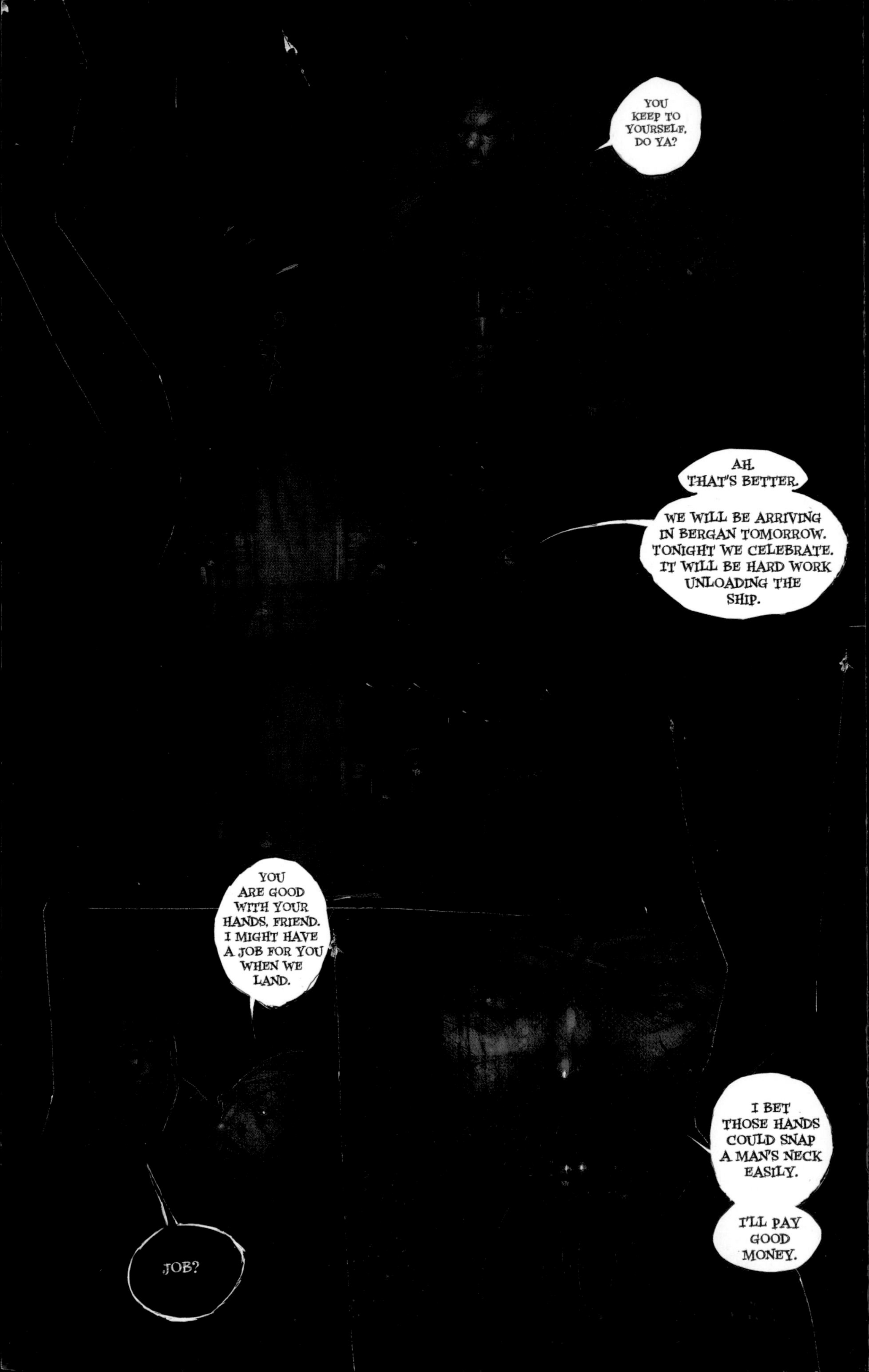
YOU KEEP TO YOURSELF, DO YA?
AH. THAT'S BETTER.
WE WILL BE ARRIVING IN BERGAN TOMORROW. TONIGHT WE CELEBRATE. IT WILL BE HARD WORK UNLOADING THE SHIP.
YOU ARE GOOD WITH YOUR HANDS, FRIEND. I MIGHT HAVE A JOB FOR YOU WHEN WE LAND.
JOB?
I BET THOSE HANDS COULD SNAP A MAN'S NECK EASILY.
I'LL PAY GOOD MONEY.

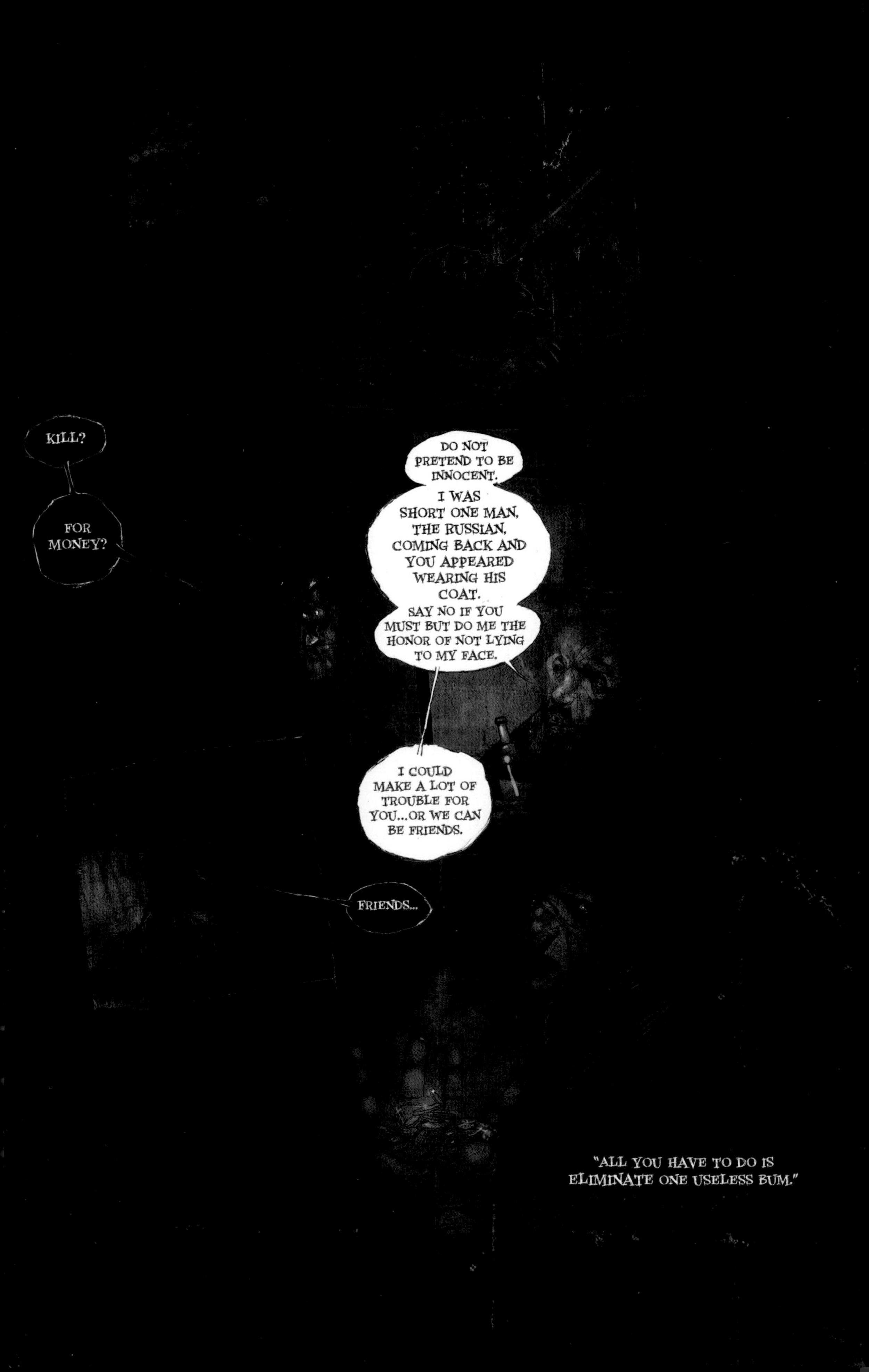
KILL?
FOR MONEY?
DO NOT PRETEND TO BE INNOCENT.
I WAS SHORT ONE MAN, THE RUSSIAN, COMING BACK AND YOU APPEARED WEARING HIS COAT.
SAY NO IF YOU MUST BUT DO ME THE HONOR OF NOT LYING TO MY FACE.
I COULD MAKE A LOT OF TROUBLE FOR YOU...OR WE CAN BE FRIENDS.
FRIENDS...
"ALL YOU HAVE TO DO IS ELIMINATE ONE USELESS BUM."

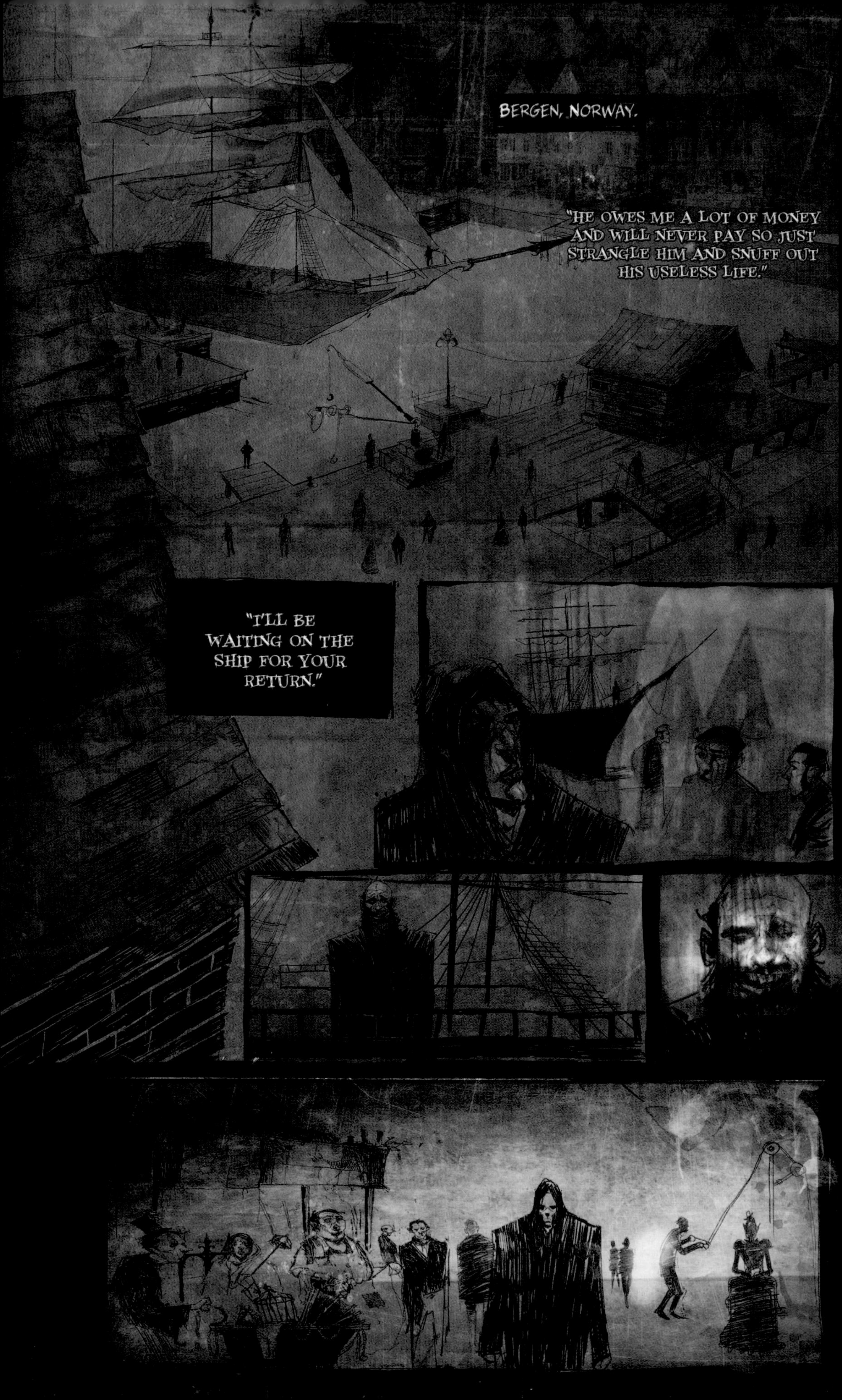
BERGEN, NORWAY.
"HE OWES ME A LOT OF MONEY AND WILL NEVER PAY SO JUST STRANGLE HIM AND SNUFF OUT HIS USELESS LIFE."
"I'LL BE WAITING ON THE SHIP FOR YOUR RETURN."

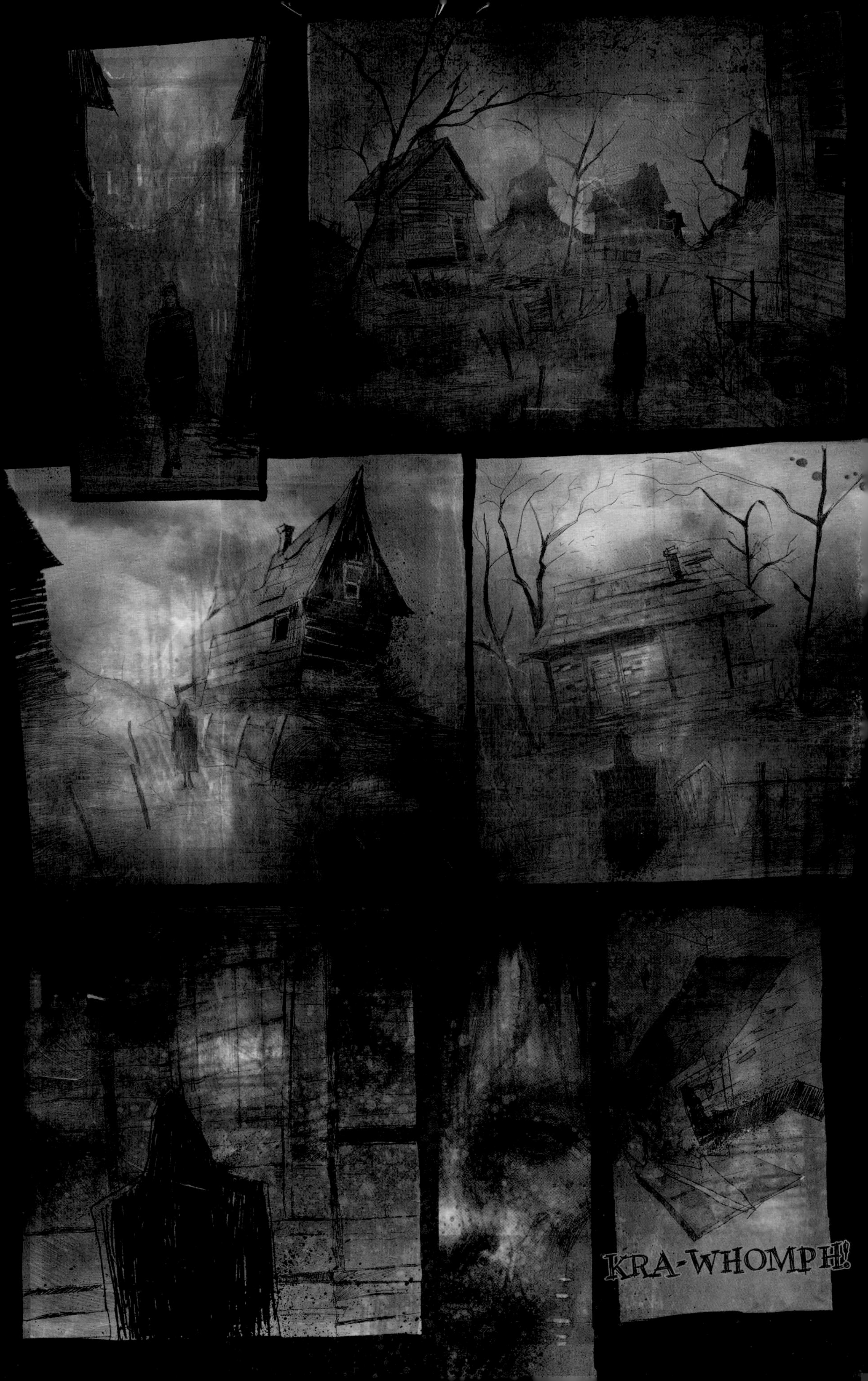
KRA-WHOMPH!

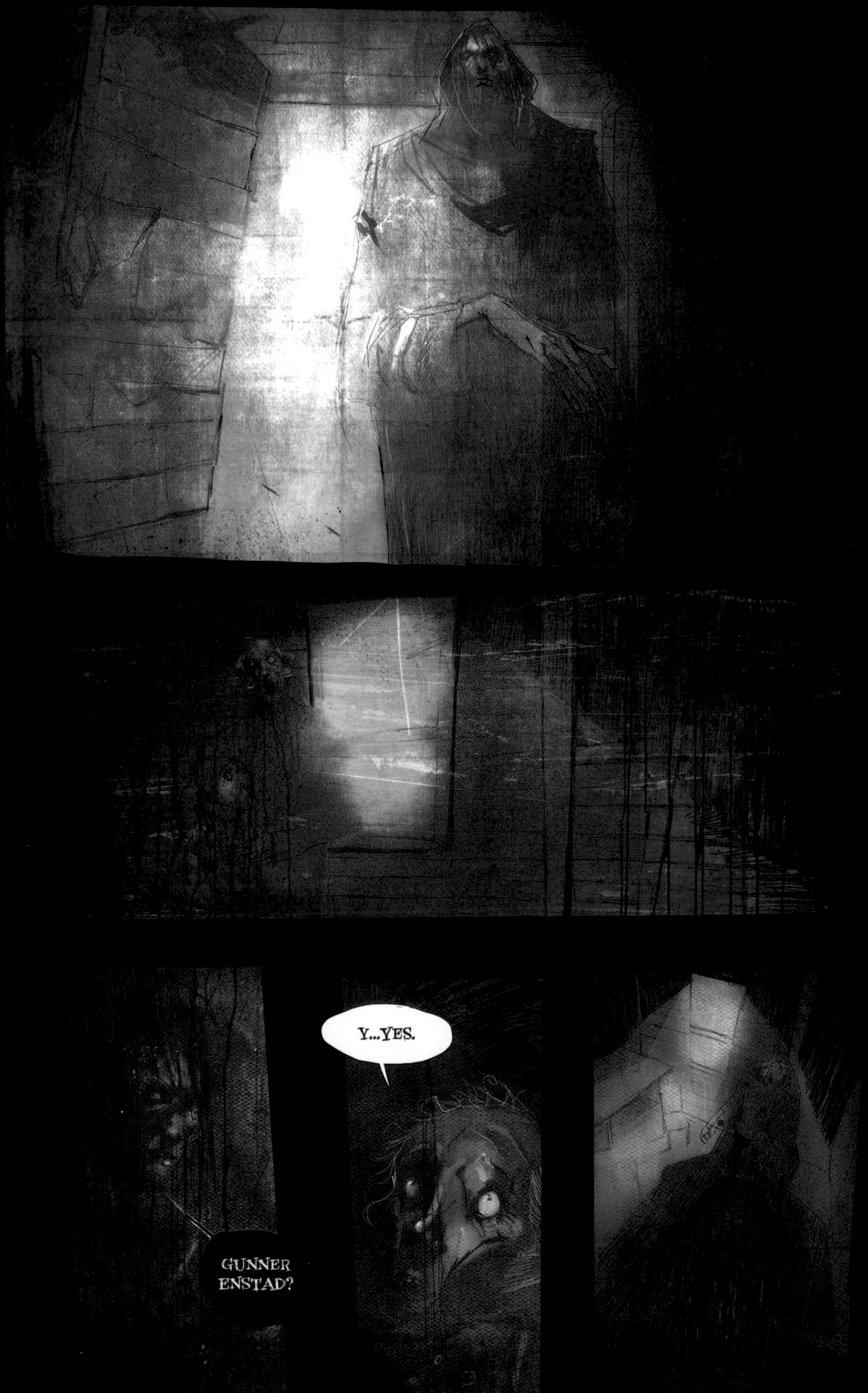
GUNNER ENSTAD?
Y...YES.

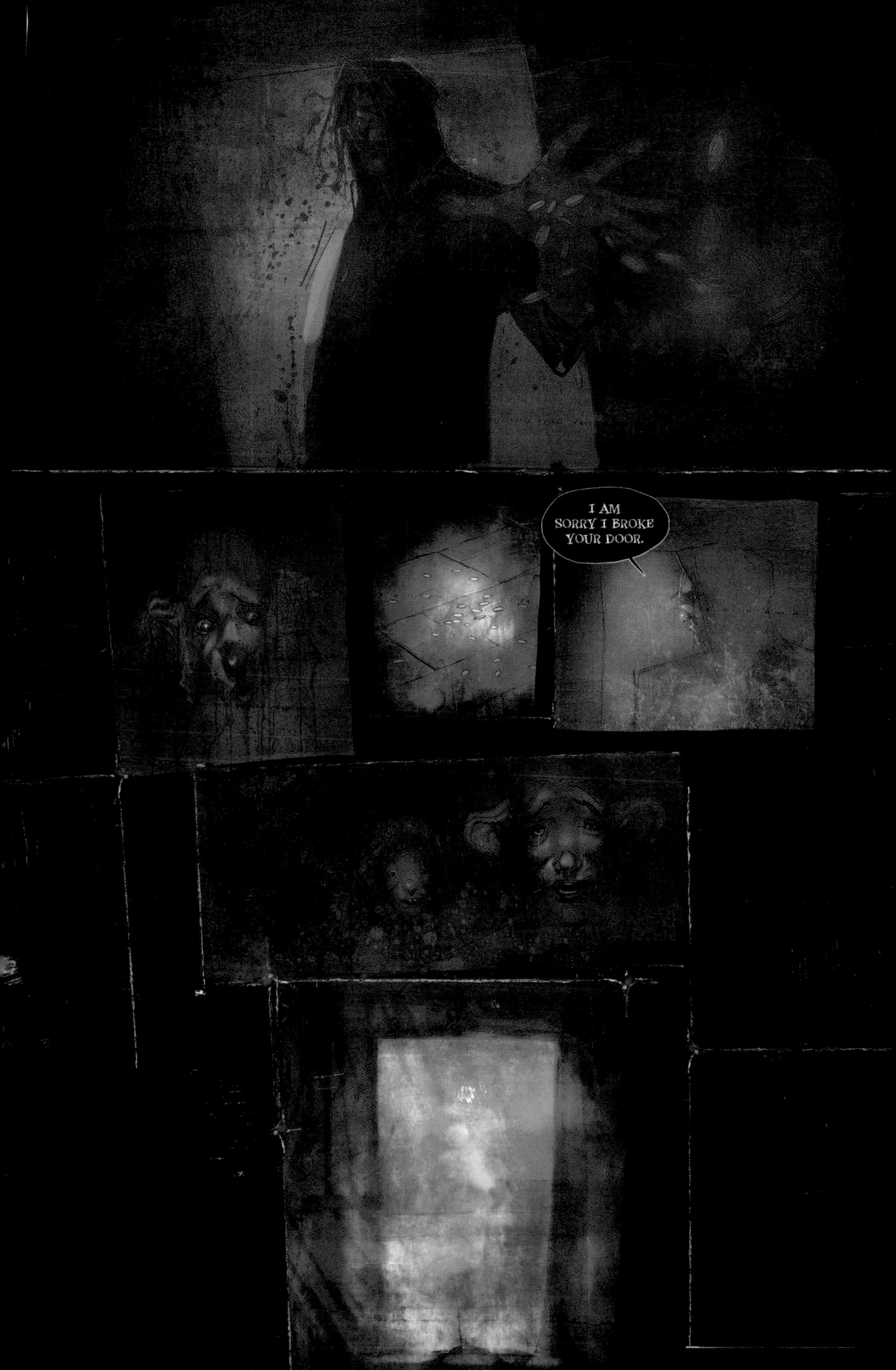
I AM SORRY I BROKE YOUR DOOR.

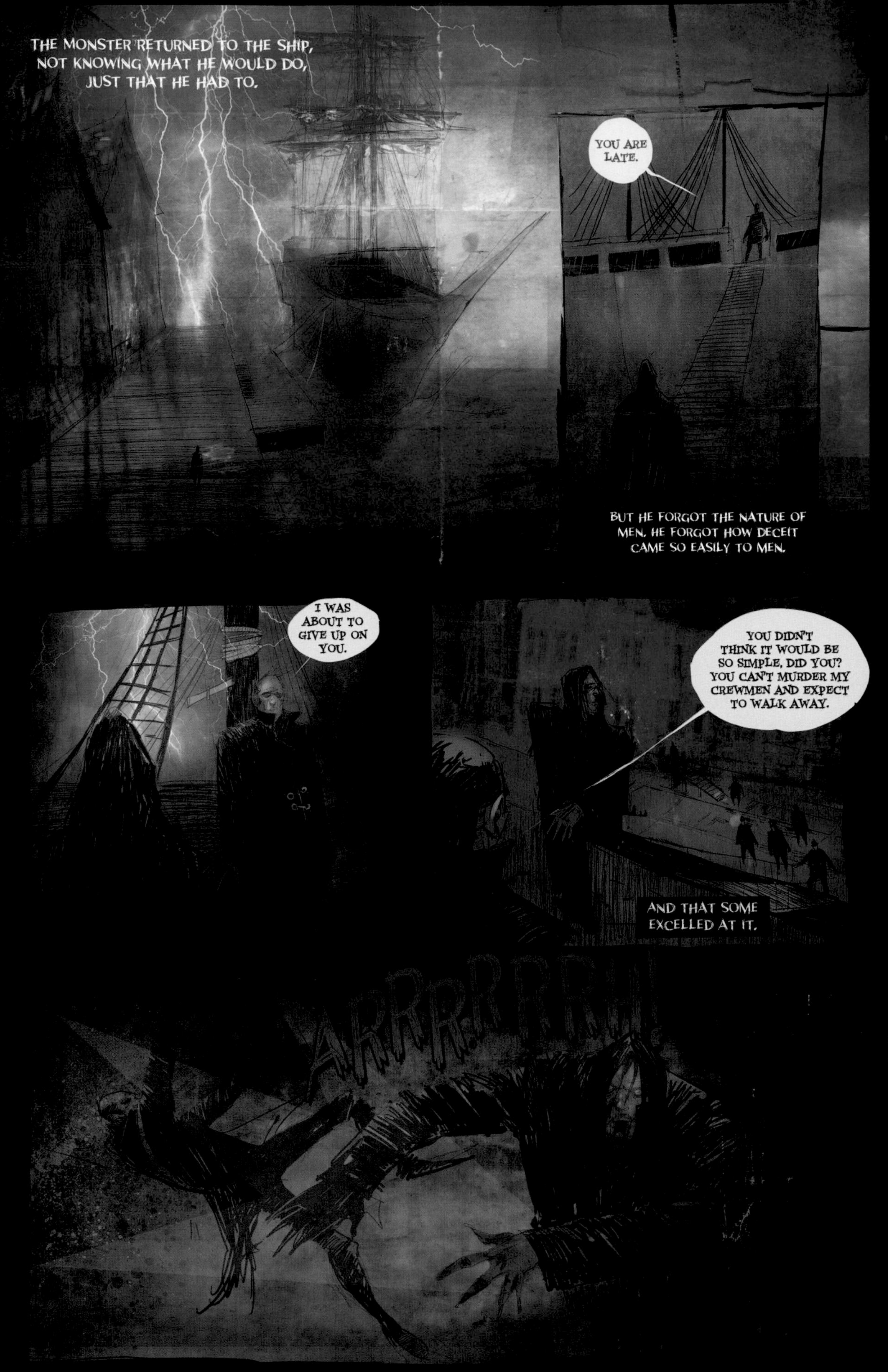
THE MONSTER RETURNED TO THE SHIP, NOT KNOWING WHAT HE WOULD DO, JUST THAT HE HAD TO.
YOU ARE LATE.
BUT HE FORGOT THE NATURE OF MEN. HE FORGOT HOW DECEIT CAME SO EASILY TO MEN.
I WAS ABOUT TO GIVE UP ON YOU.
YOU DIDN'T THINK IT WOULD BE SO SIMPLE, DID YOU? YOU CAN'T MURDER MY CREWMEN AND EXPECT TO WALK AWAY.
AND THAT SOME EXCELLED AT IT.
ARRRRRRH!

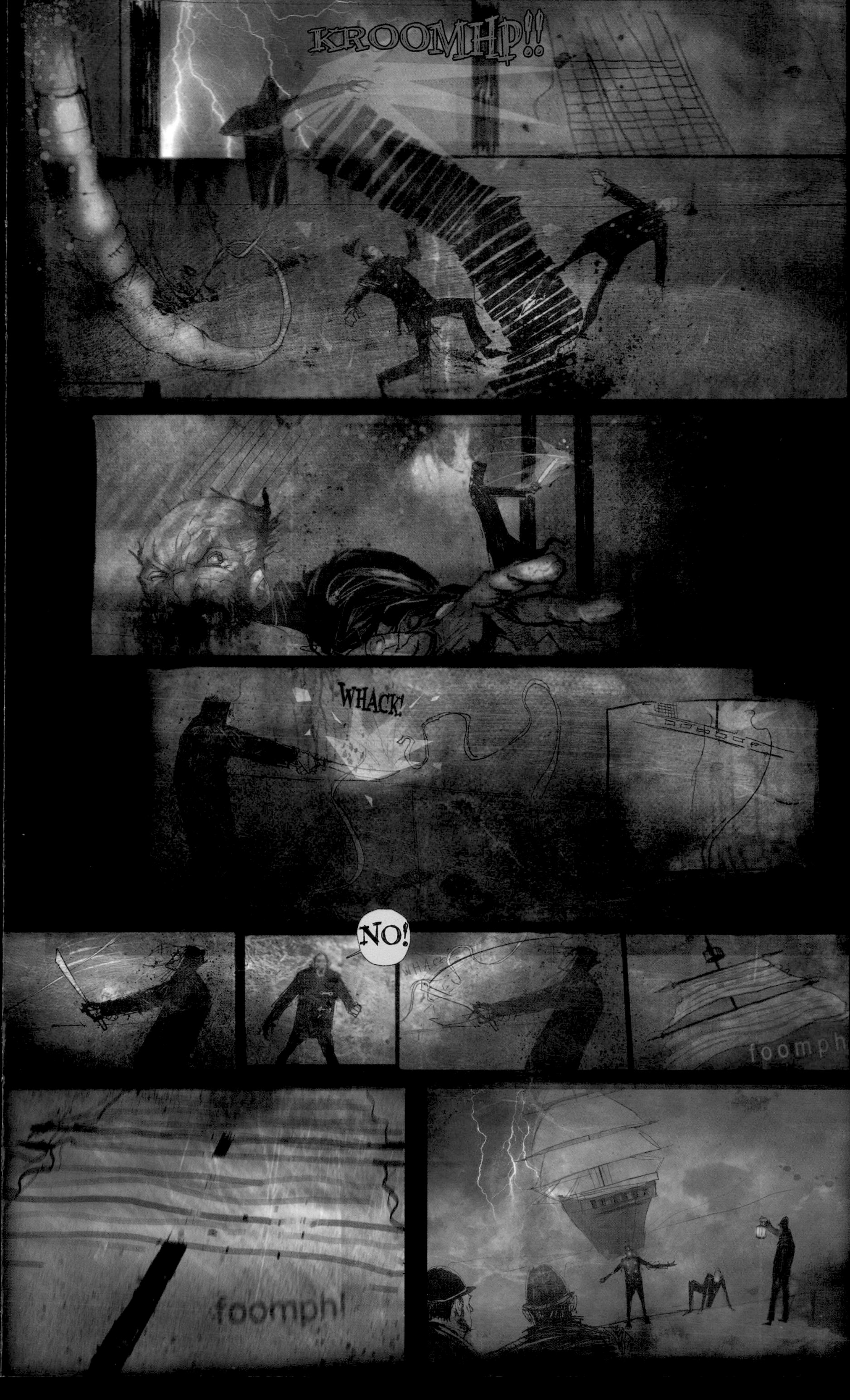
KROOMHP!!
WHACK!
NO!
WHACK
foomph
foomph!

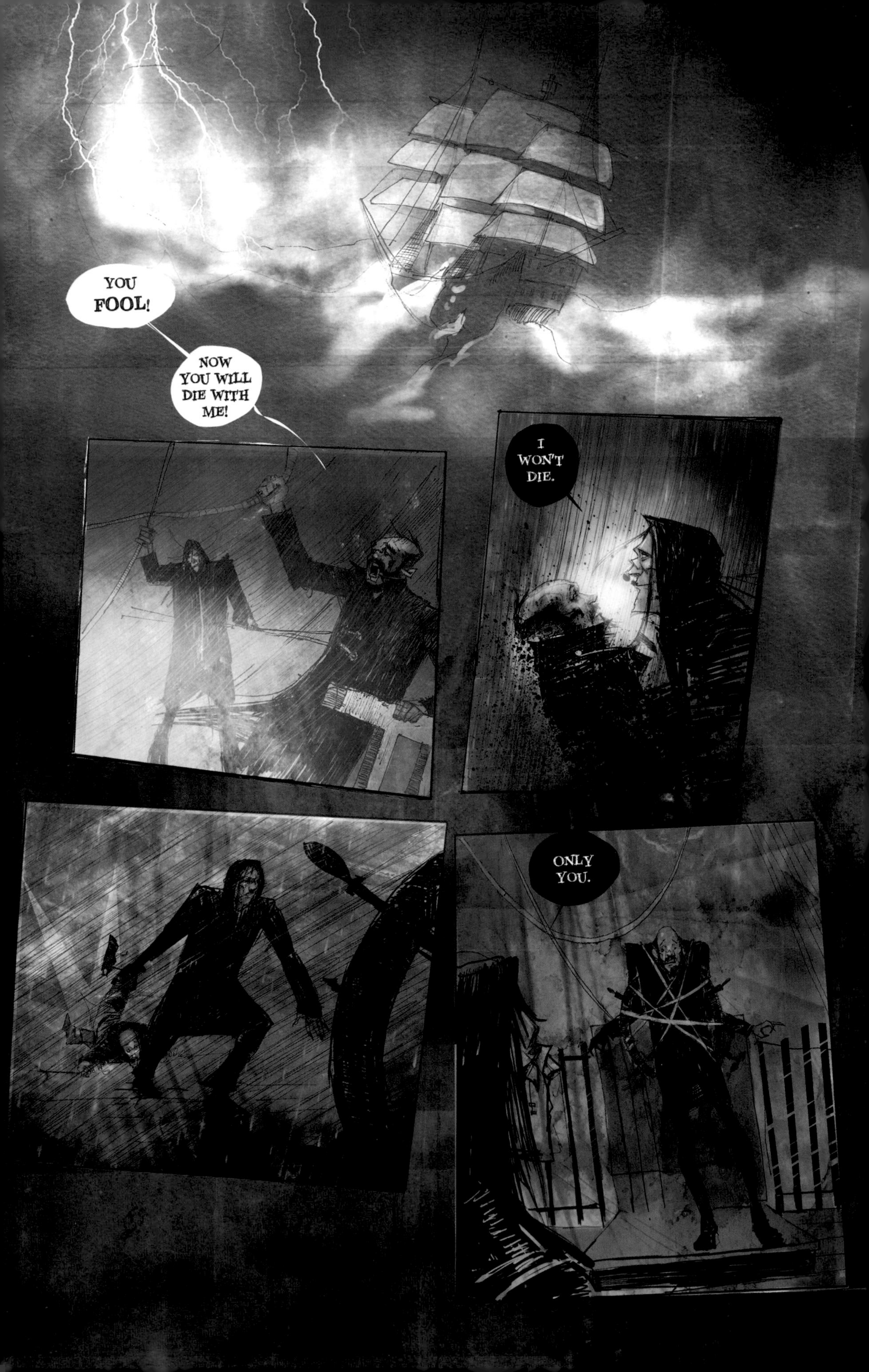
YOU FOOL!
NOW YOU WILL DIE WITH ME!
I WON'T DIE.
ONLY YOU.

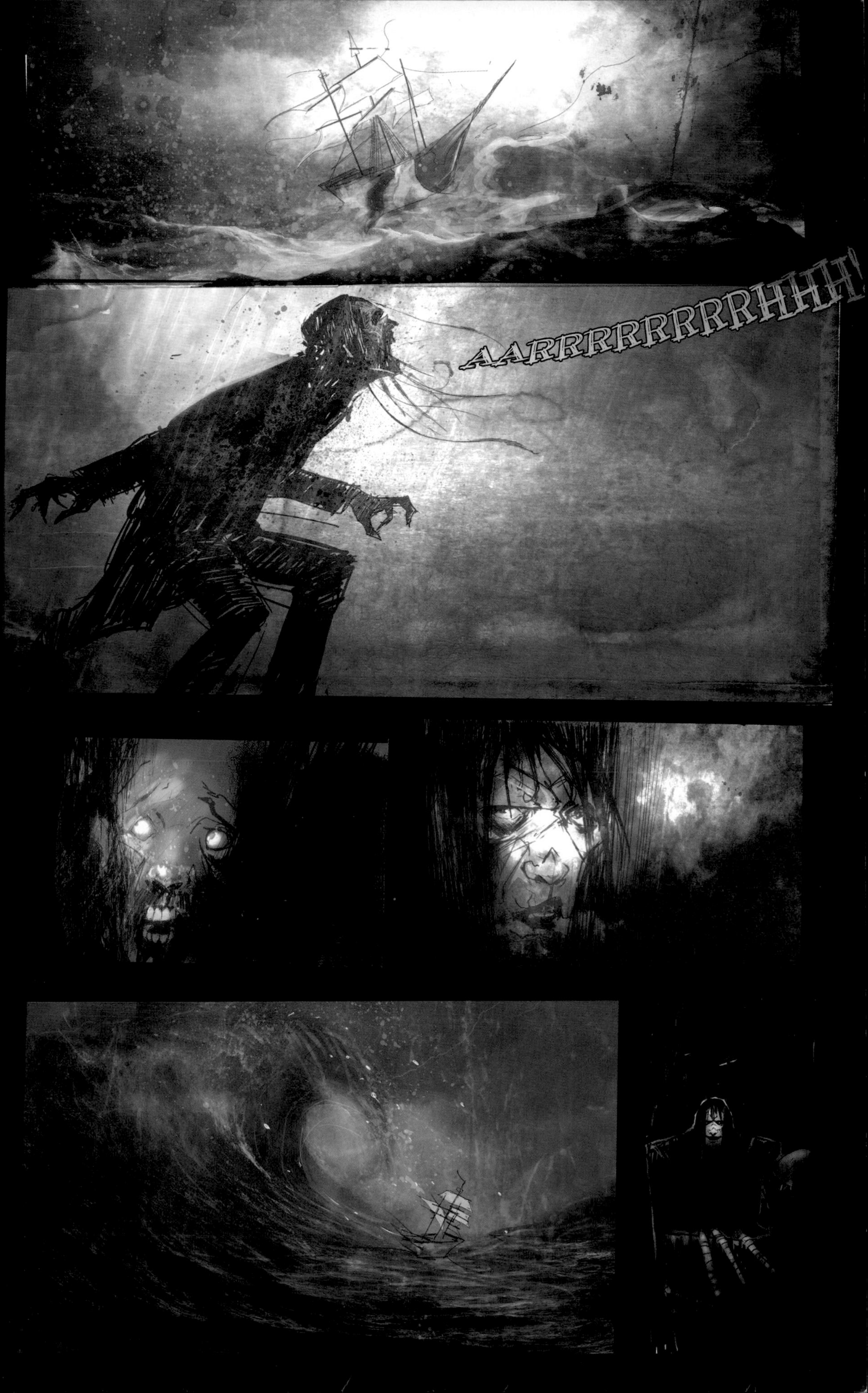
AARRRRRRRRRHHH!

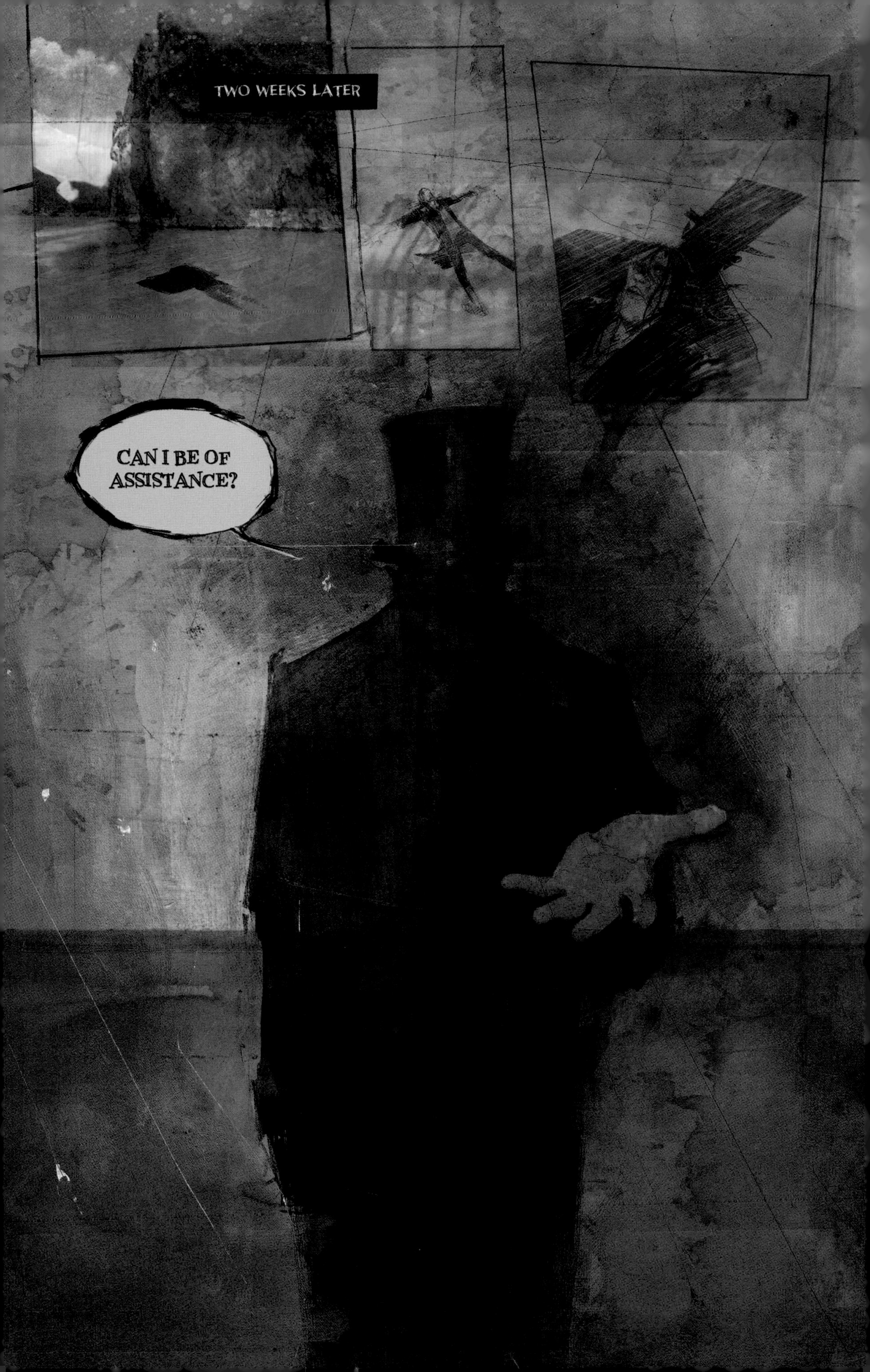
TWO WEEKS LATER
CAN I BE OF ASSISTANCE?

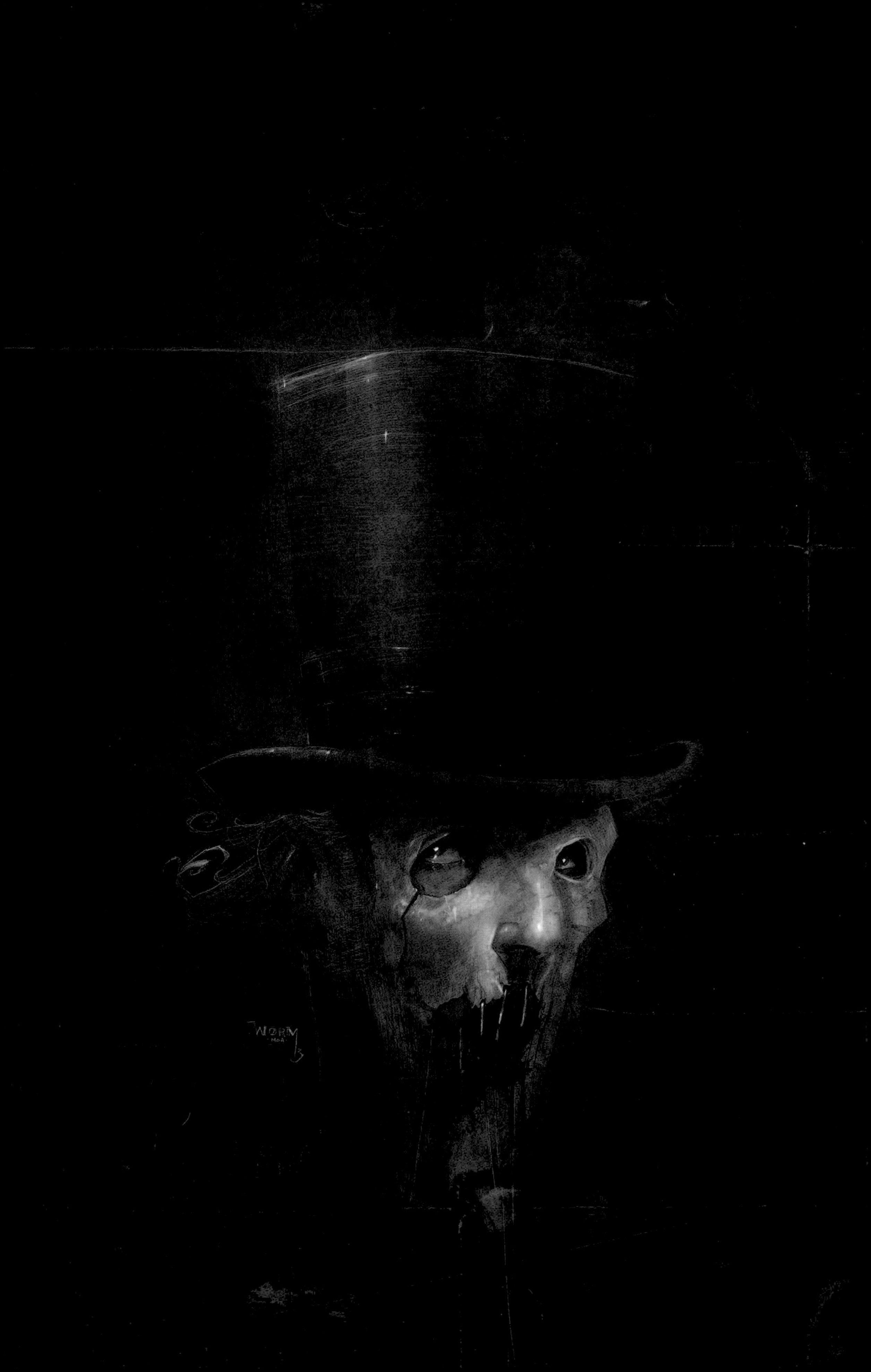

UHHHH.
WHERE AM I?

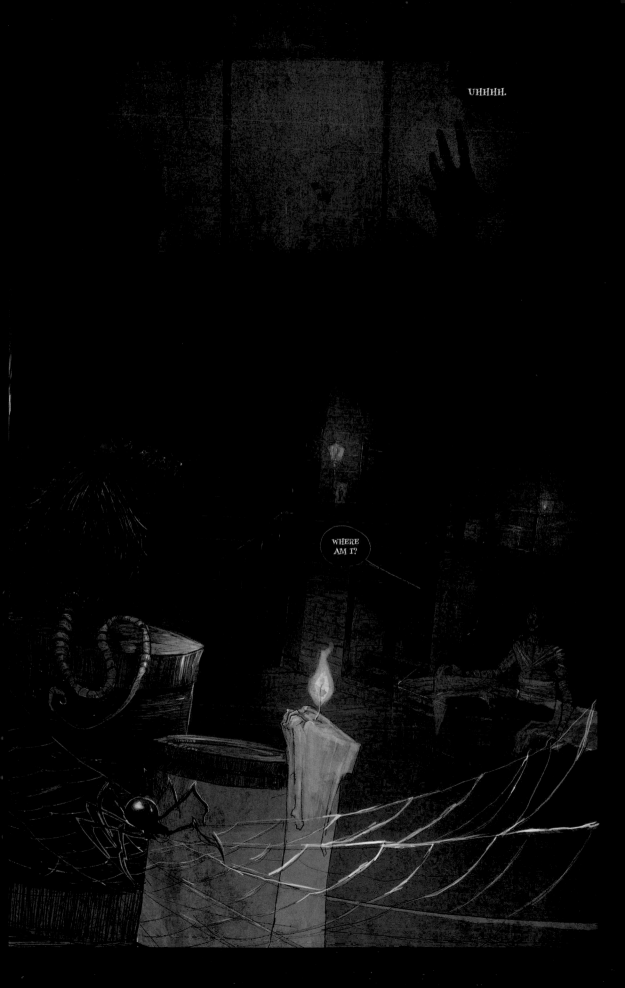

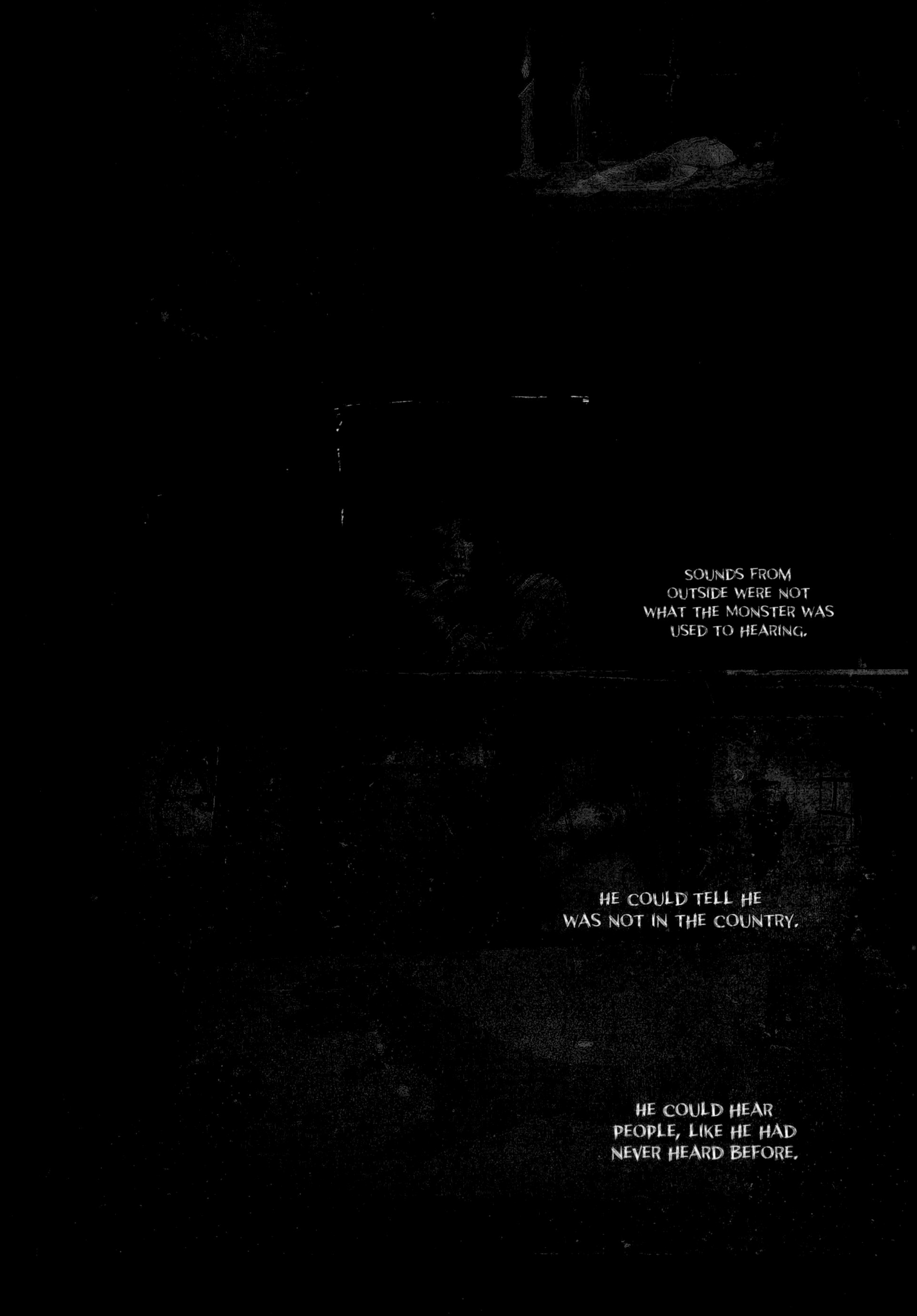
SOUNDS FROM OUTSIDE WERE NOT WHAT THE MONSTER WAS USED TO HEARING.
HE COULD TELL HE WAS NOT IN THE COUNTRY.
HE COULD HEAR PEOPLE, LIKE HE HAD NEVER HEARD BEFORE.

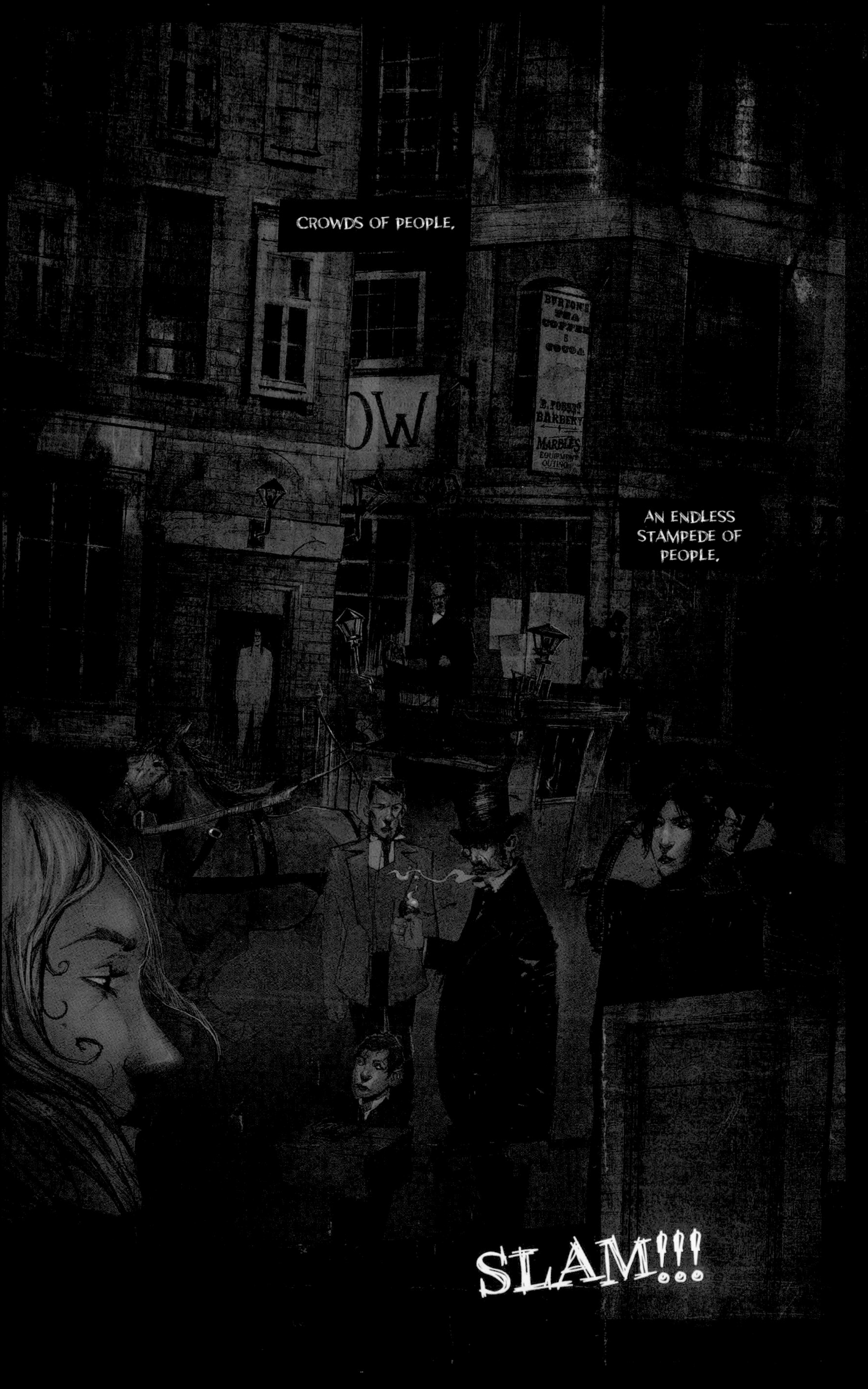
CROWDS OF PEOPLE,
AN ENDLESS STAMPEDE OF PEOPLE,
SLAM!!!

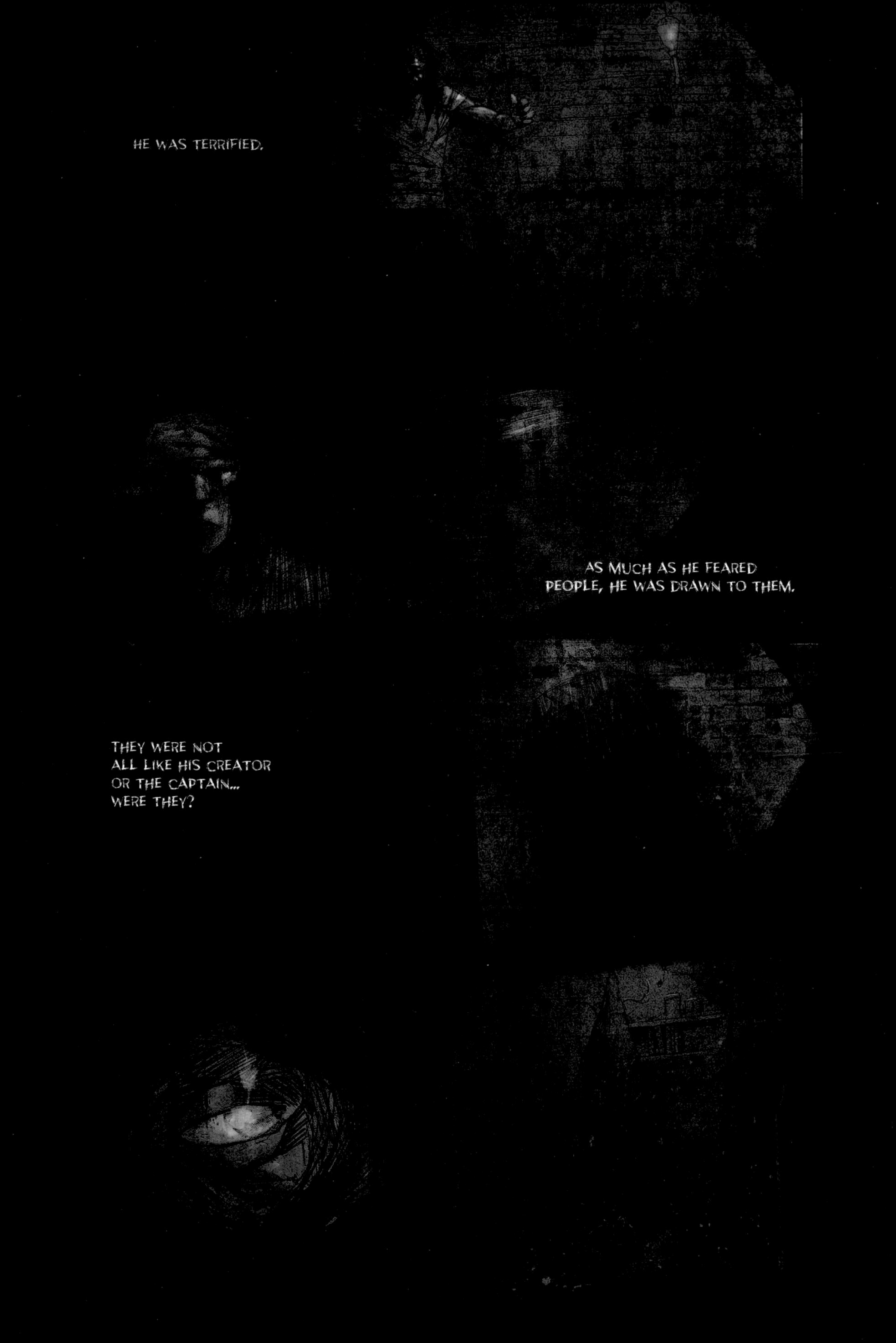
HE WAS TERRIFIED.
AS MUCH AS HE FEARED PEOPLE, HE WAS DRAWN TO THEM.
THEY WERE NOT ALL LIKE HIS CREATOR OR THE CAPTAIN... WERE THEY?

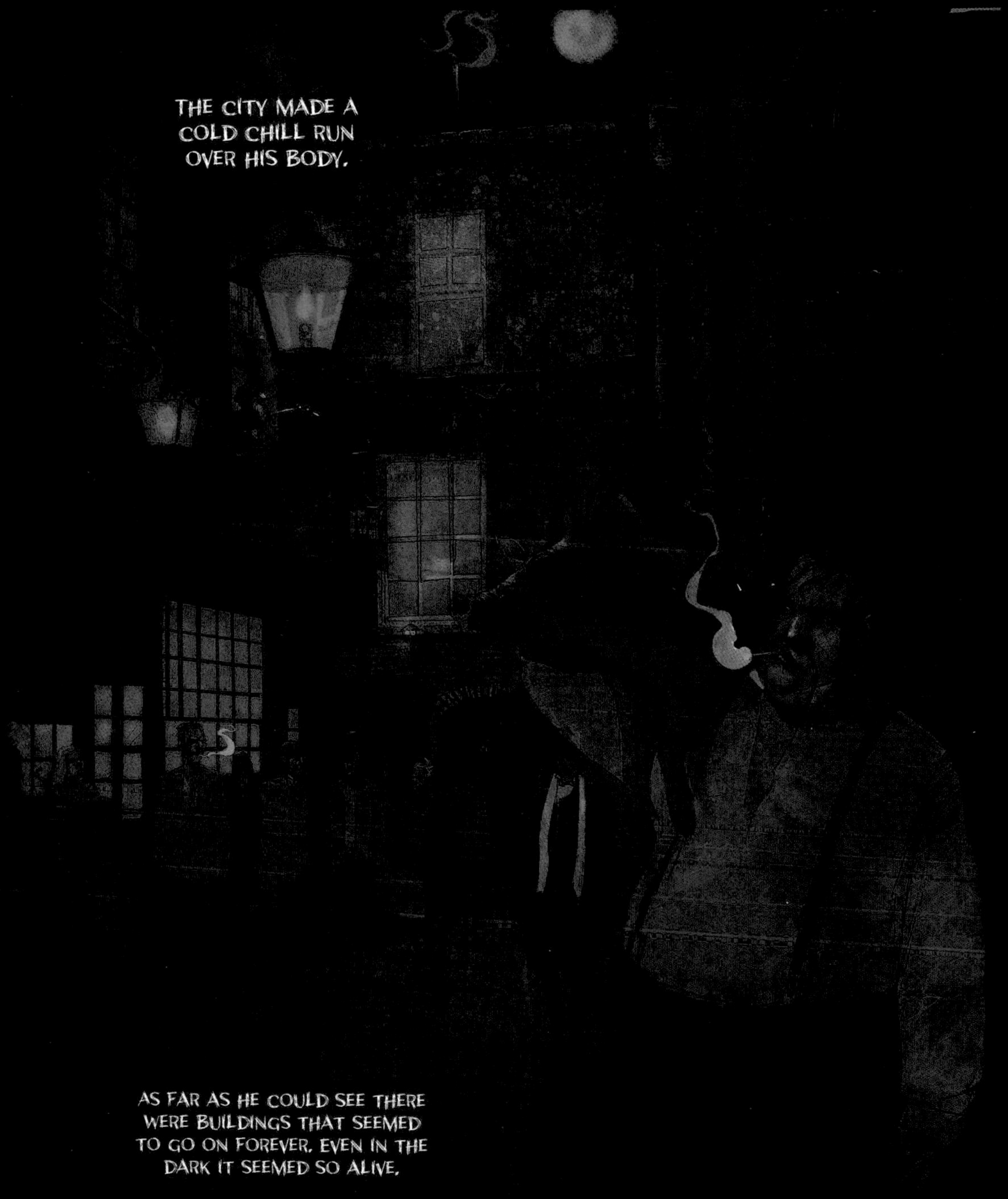
THE CITY MADE A COLD CHILL RUN OVER HIS BODY.
AS FAR AS HE COULD SEE THERE WERE BUILDINGS THAT SEEMED TO GO ON FOREVER. EVEN IN THE DARK IT SEEMED SO ALIVE.
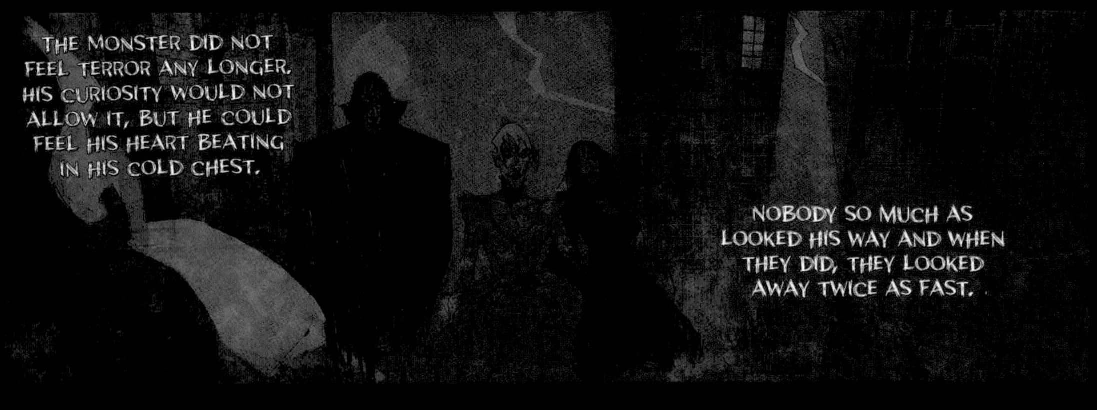
THE MONSTER DID NOT FEEL TERROR ANY LONGER. HIS CURIOSITY WOULD NOT ALLOW IT, BUT HE COULD FEEL HIS HEART BEATING IN HIS COLD CHEST.
NOBODY SO MUCH AS LOOKED HIS WAY AND WHEN THEY DID, THEY LOOKED AWAY TWICE AS FAST.

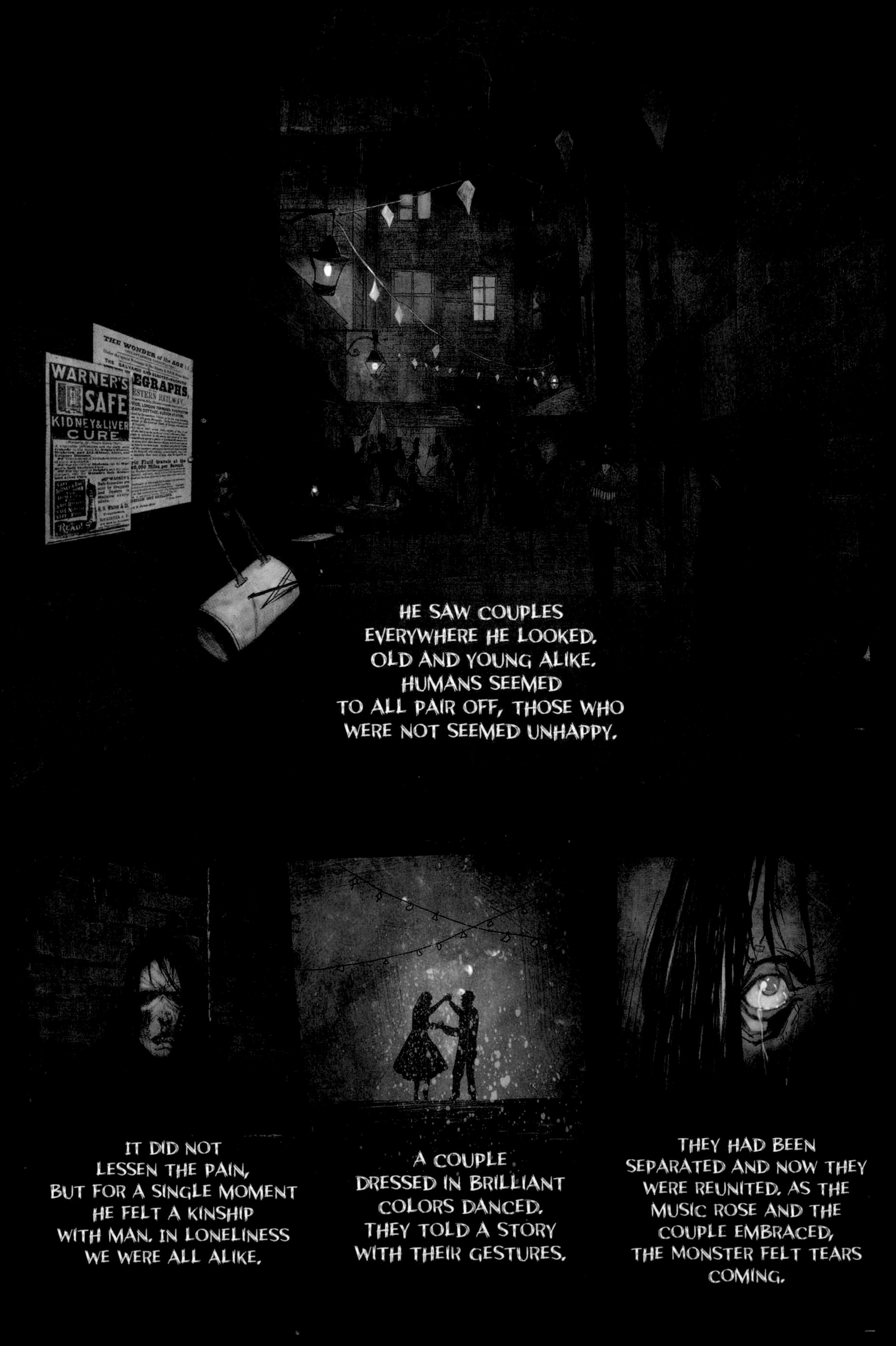
WARNER'S
SAFE
KIDNEY&LIVER
CURE
HE SAW COUPLES EVERYWHERE HE LOOKED. OLD AND YOUNG ALIKE. HUMANS SEEMED TO ALL PAIR OFF, THOSE WHO WERE NOT SEEMED UNHAPPY.
IT DID NOT LESSEN THE PAIN, BUT FOR A SINGLE MOMENT HE FELT A KINSHIP WITH MAN. IN LONELINESS WE WERE ALL ALIKE.
A COUPLE DRESSED IN BRILLIANT COLORS DANCED. THEY TOLD A STORY WITH THEIR GESTURES.
THEY HAD BEEN SEPARATED AND NOW THEY WERE REUNITED. AS THE MUSIC ROSE AND THE COUPLE EMBRACED, THE MONSTER FELT TEARS COMING.

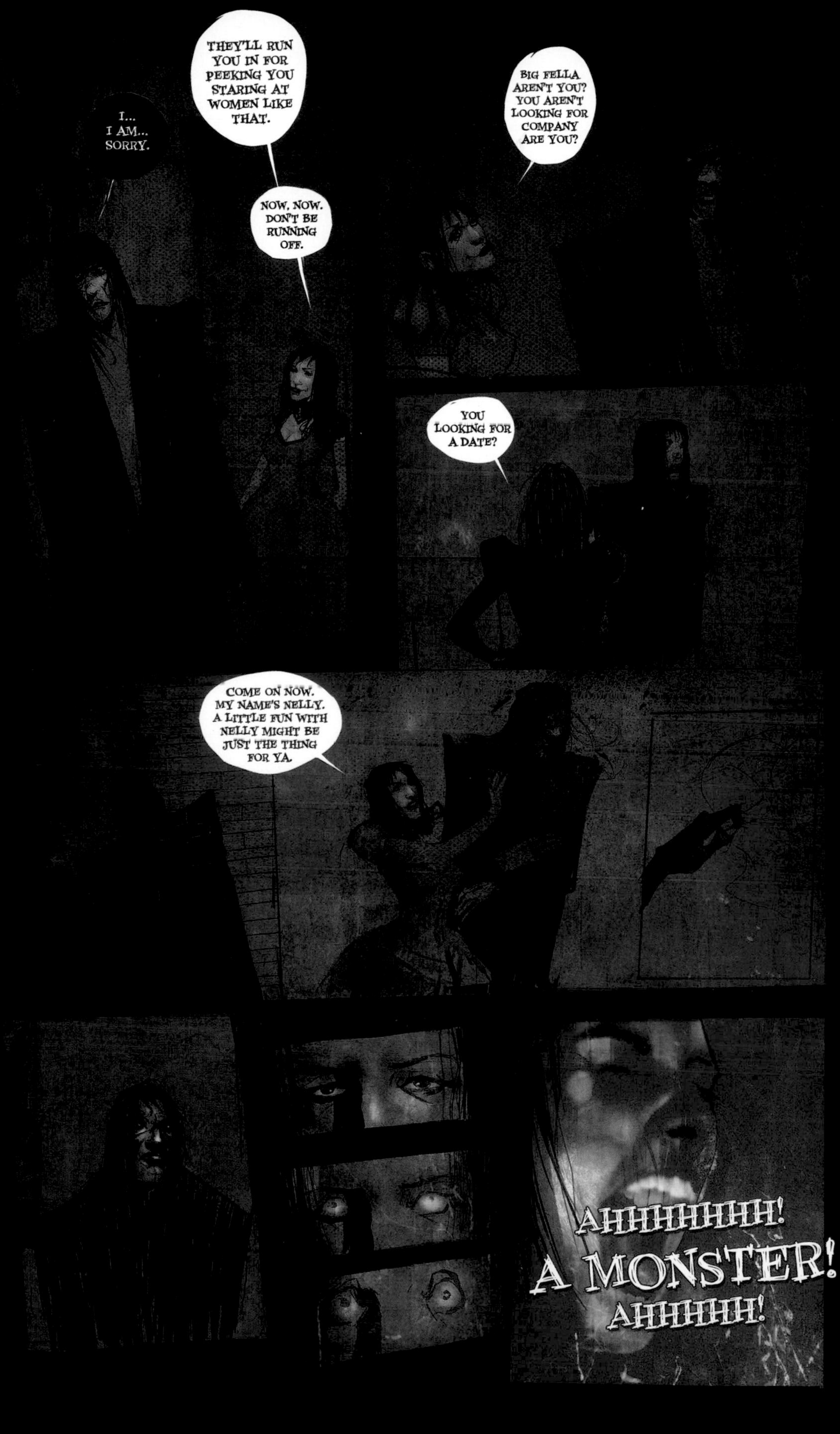
I... I AM... SORRY.
THEY'LL RUN YOU IN FOR PEEKING YOU STARING AT WOMEN LIKE THAT.
NOW, NOW. DON'T BE RUNNING OFF.
BIG FELLA AREN'T YOU? YOU AREN'T LOOKING FOR COMPANY ARE YOU?
YOU LOOKING FOR A DATE?
COME ON NOW. MY NAME'S NELLY. A LITTLE FUN WITH NELLY MIGHT BE JUST THE THING FOR YA.
AHHHHHHH! A MONSTER! AHHHHH!

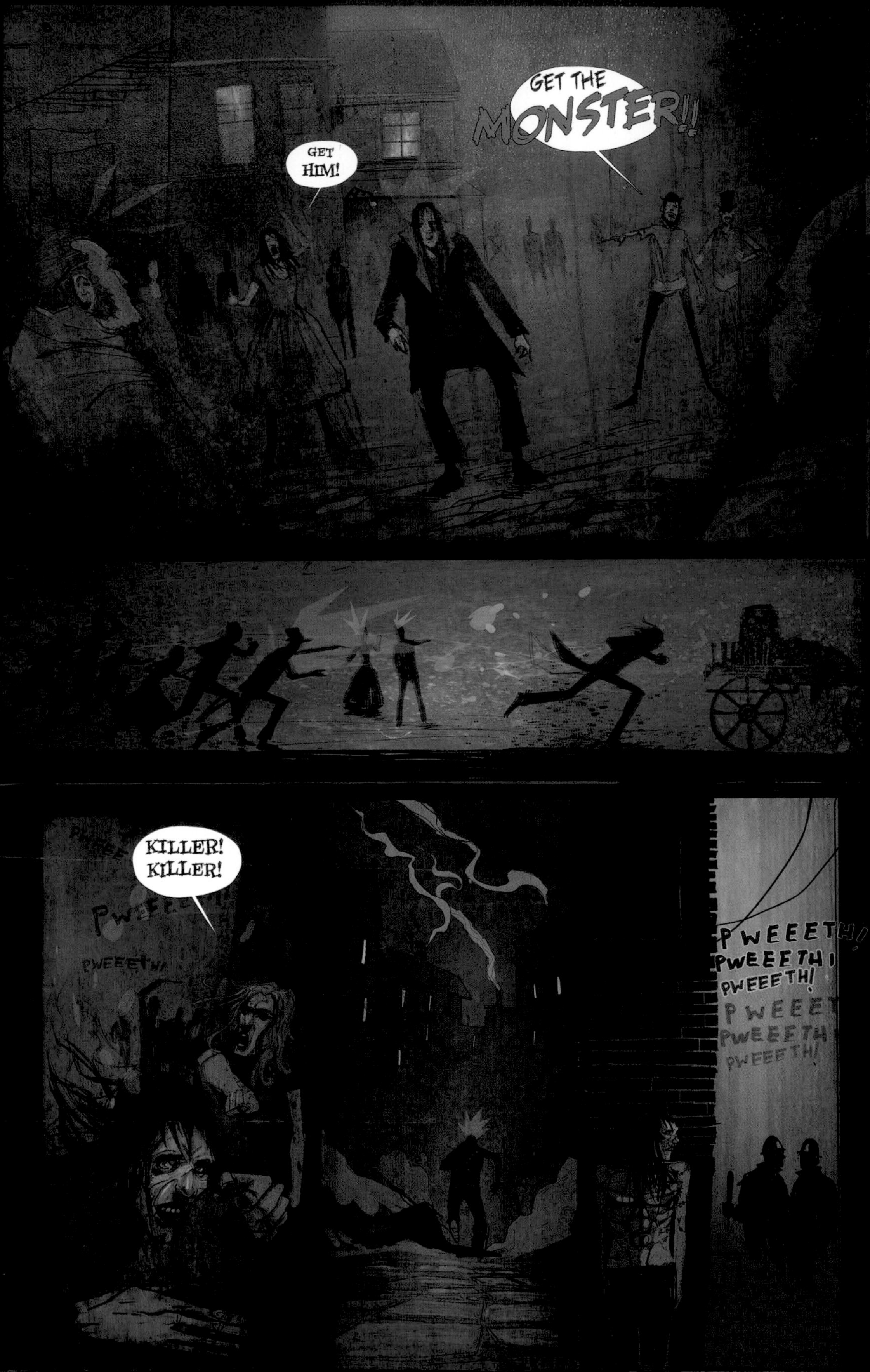
GET HIM!
GET THE MONSTER!!
KILLER! KILLER!
PWEEETH!
PWEEETH!
PWEEETH!
PWEEETH!
PWEEETH!

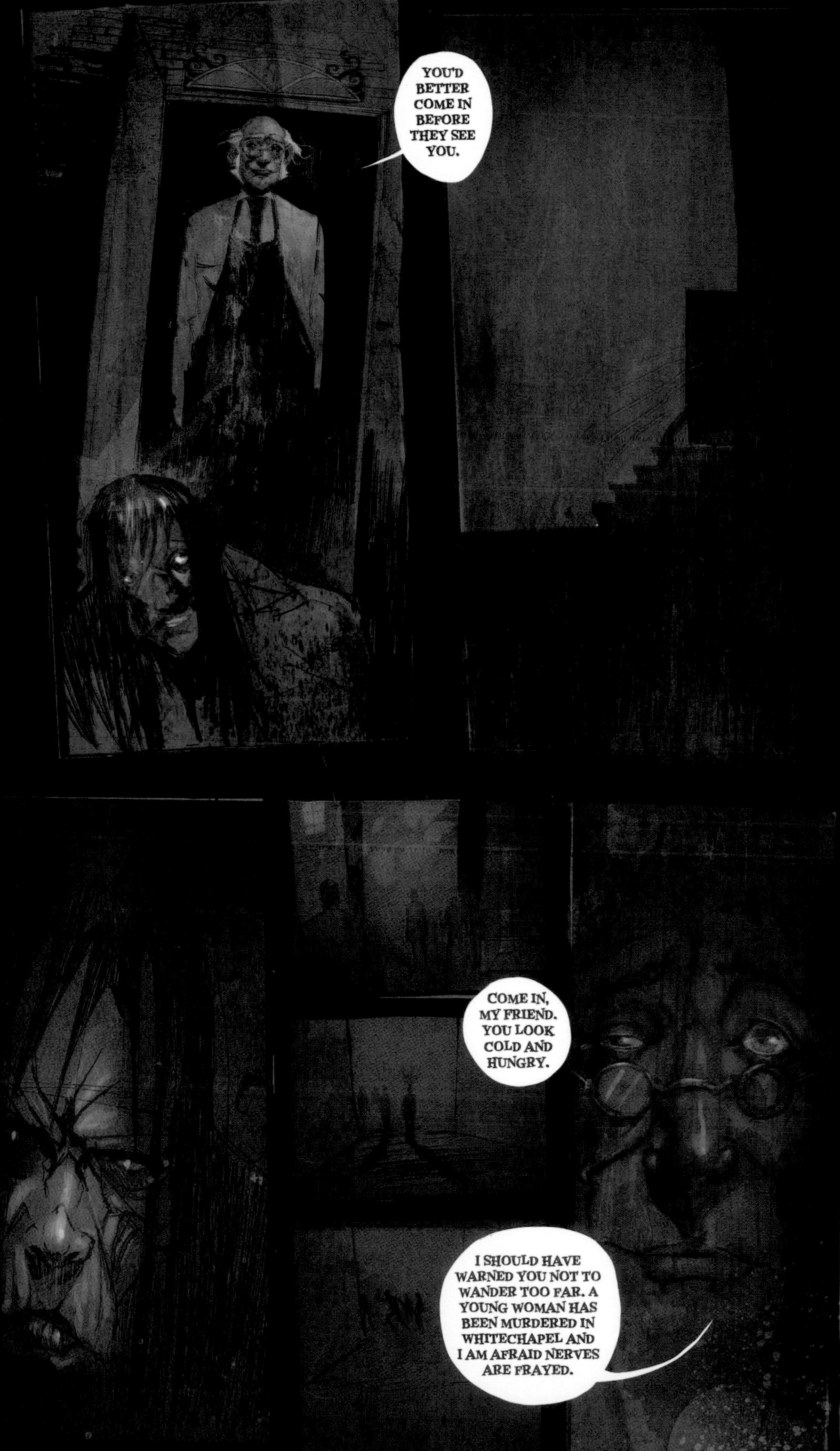
YOU'D BETTER COME IN BEFORE THEY SEE YOU.
COME IN, MY FRIEND. YOU LOOK COLD AND HUNGRY.
I SHOULD HAVE WARNED YOU NOT TO WANDER TOO FAR. A YOUNG WOMAN HAS BEEN MURDERED IN WHITECHAPEL AND I AM AFRAID NERVES ARE FRAYED.

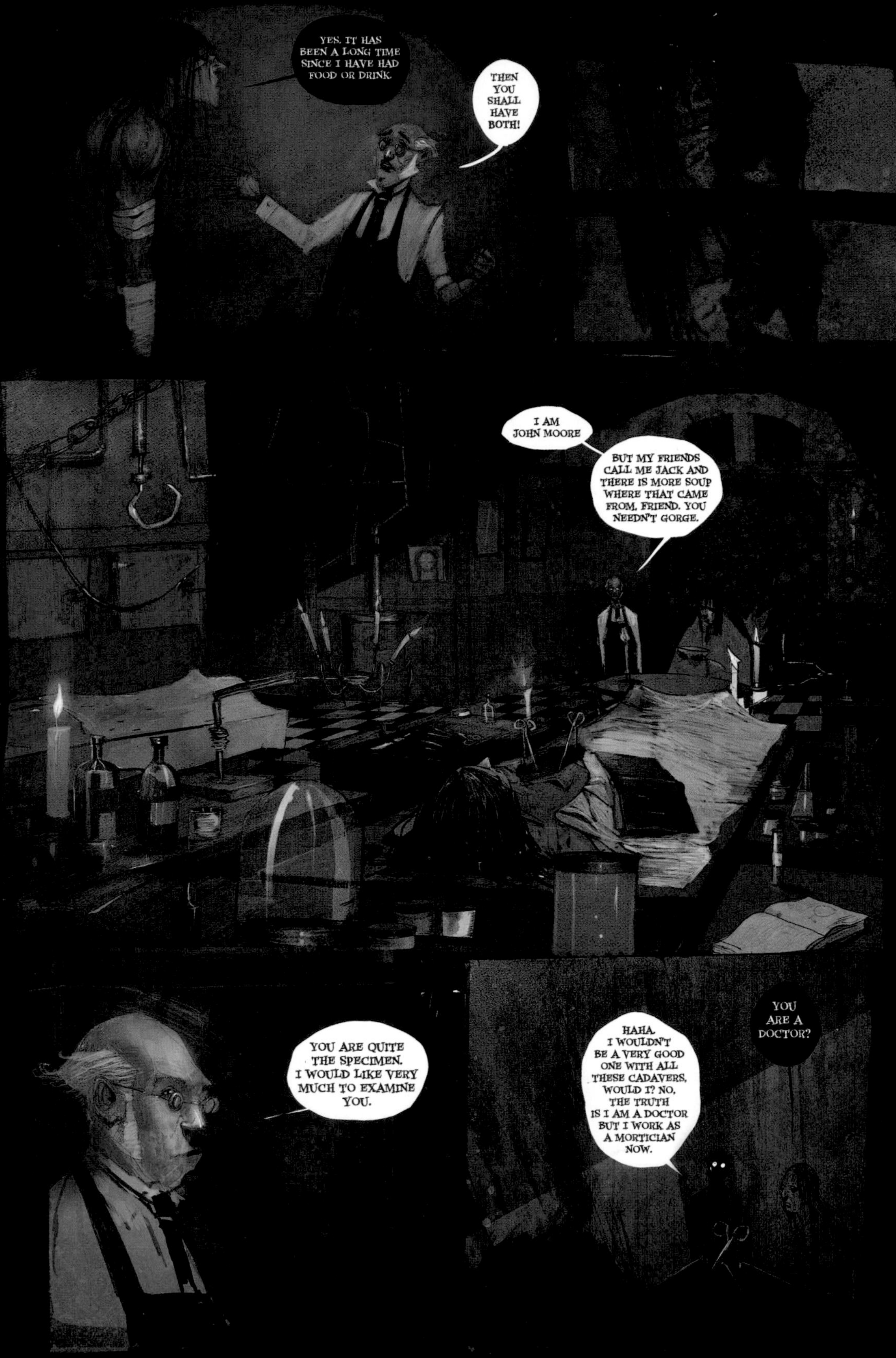
YES. IT HAS BEEN A LONG TIME SINCE I HAVE HAD FOOD OR DRINK.
THEN YOU SHALL HAVE BOTH!
I AM JOHN MOORE
BUT MY FRIENDS CALL ME JACK AND THERE IS MORE SOUP WHERE THAT CAME FROM, FRIEND. YOU NEEDN'T GORGE.
YOU ARE QUITE THE SPECIMEN. I WOULD LIKE VERY MUCH TO EXAMINE YOU.
YOU ARE A DOCTOR?
HAHA. I WOULDN'T BE A VERY GOOD ONE WITH ALL THESE CADAVERS, WOULD I? NO, THE TRUTH IS I AM A DOCTOR BUT I WORK AS A MORTICIAN NOW.

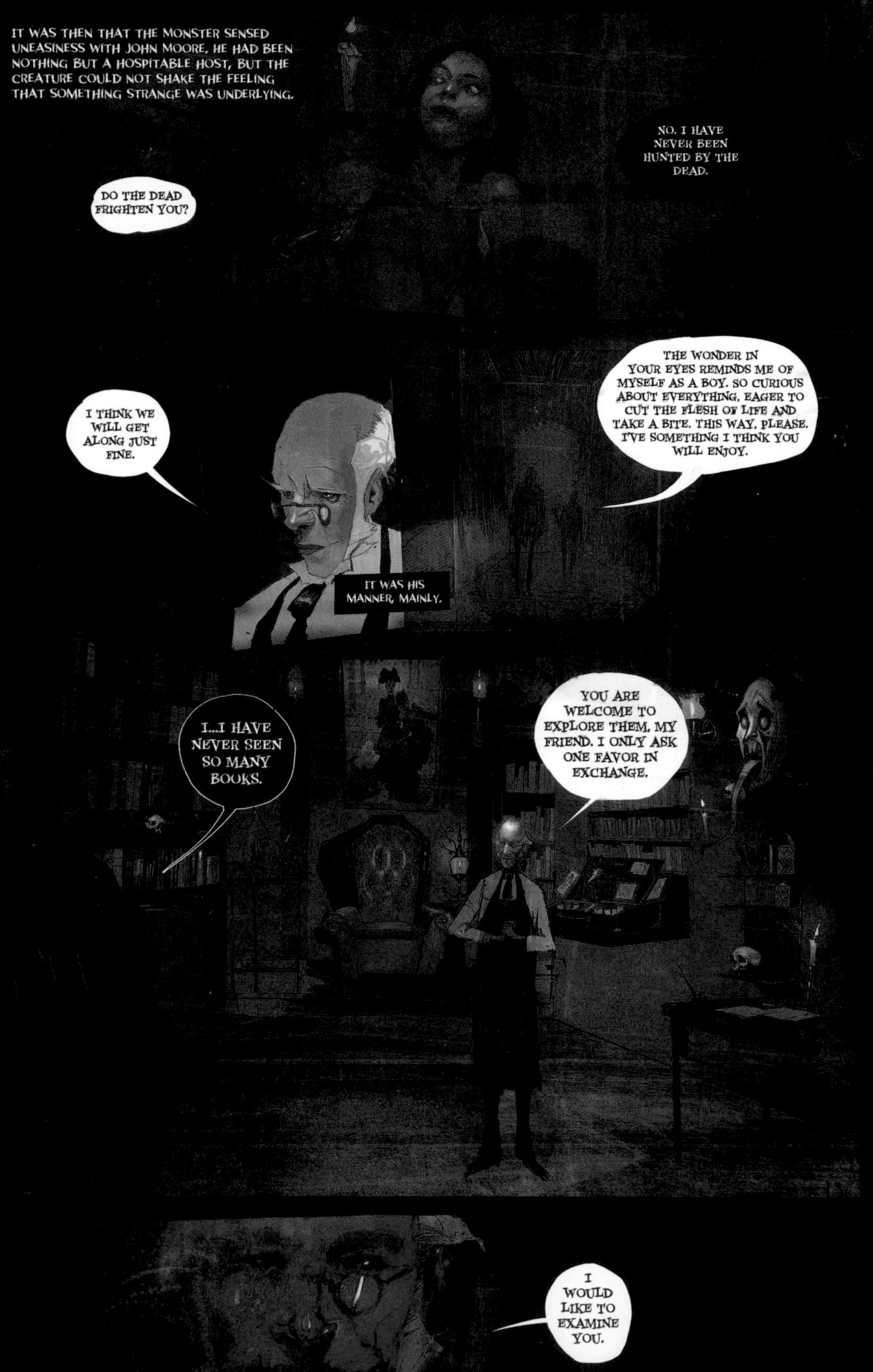

IT WAS THEN THAT THE MONSTER SENSED UNEASINESS WITH JOHN MOORE. HE HAD BEEN NOTHING BUT A HOSPITABLE HOST, BUT THE CREATURE COULD NOT SHAKE THE FEELING THAT SOMETHING STRANGE WAS UNDERLYING.
DO THE DEAD FRIGHTEN YOU?
NO. I HAVE NEVER BEEN HUNTED BY THE DEAD.
I THINK WE WILL GET ALONG JUST FINE.
THE WONDER IN YOUR EYES REMINDS ME OF MYSELF AS A BOY. SO CURIOUS ABOUT EVERYTHING, EAGER TO CUT THE FLESH OF LIFE AND TAKE A BITE. THIS WAY, PLEASE. I'VE SOMETHING I THINK YOU WILL ENJOY.
IT WAS HIS MANNER, MAINLY.
I...I HAVE NEVER SEEN SO MANY BOOKS.
YOU ARE WELCOME TO EXPLORE THEM, MY FRIEND. I ONLY ASK ONE FAVOR IN EXCHANGE.
I WOULD LIKE TO EXAMINE YOU.

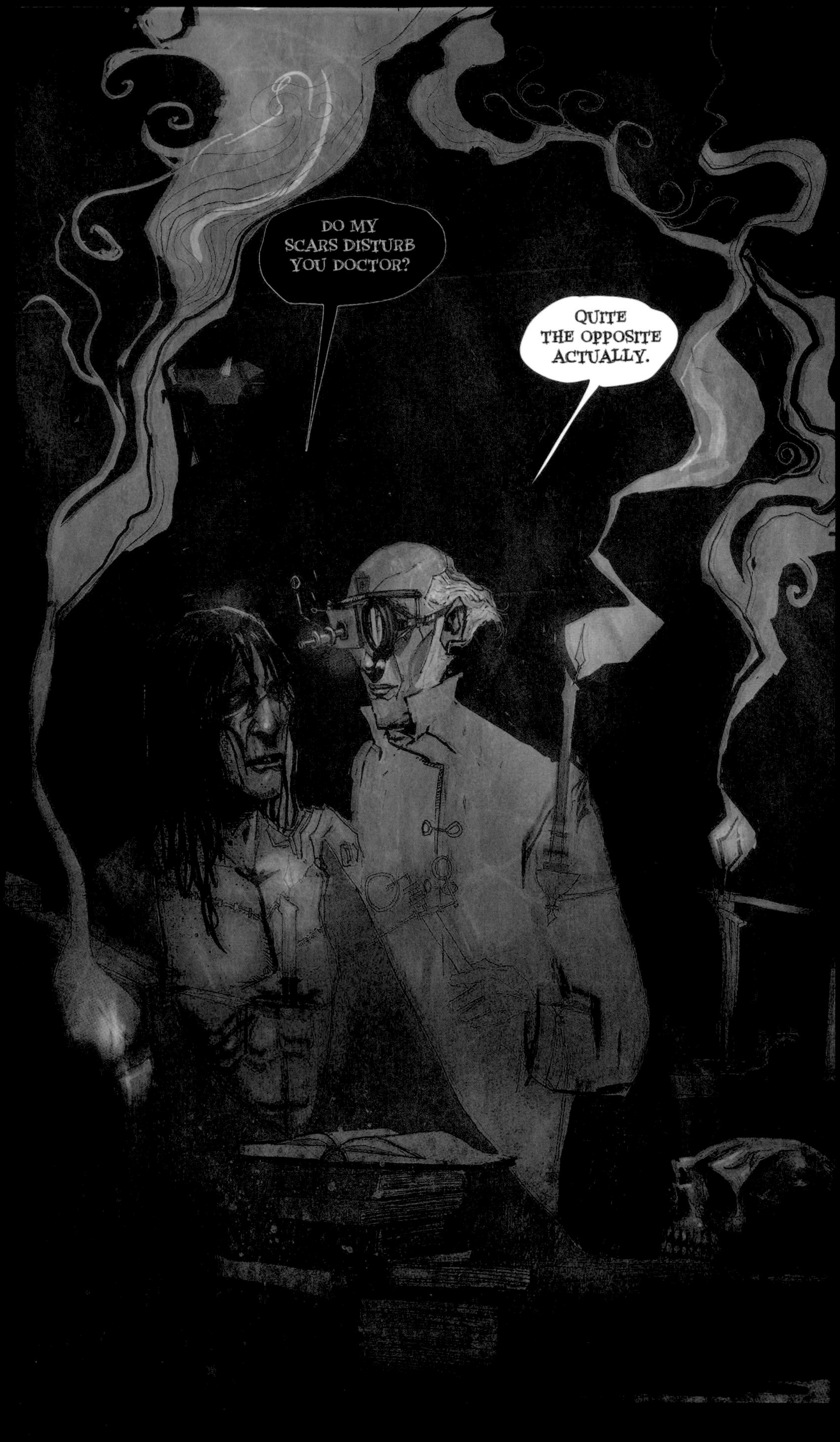
DO MY SCARS DISTURB YOU DOCTOR?
QUITE THE OPPOSITE ACTUALLY.

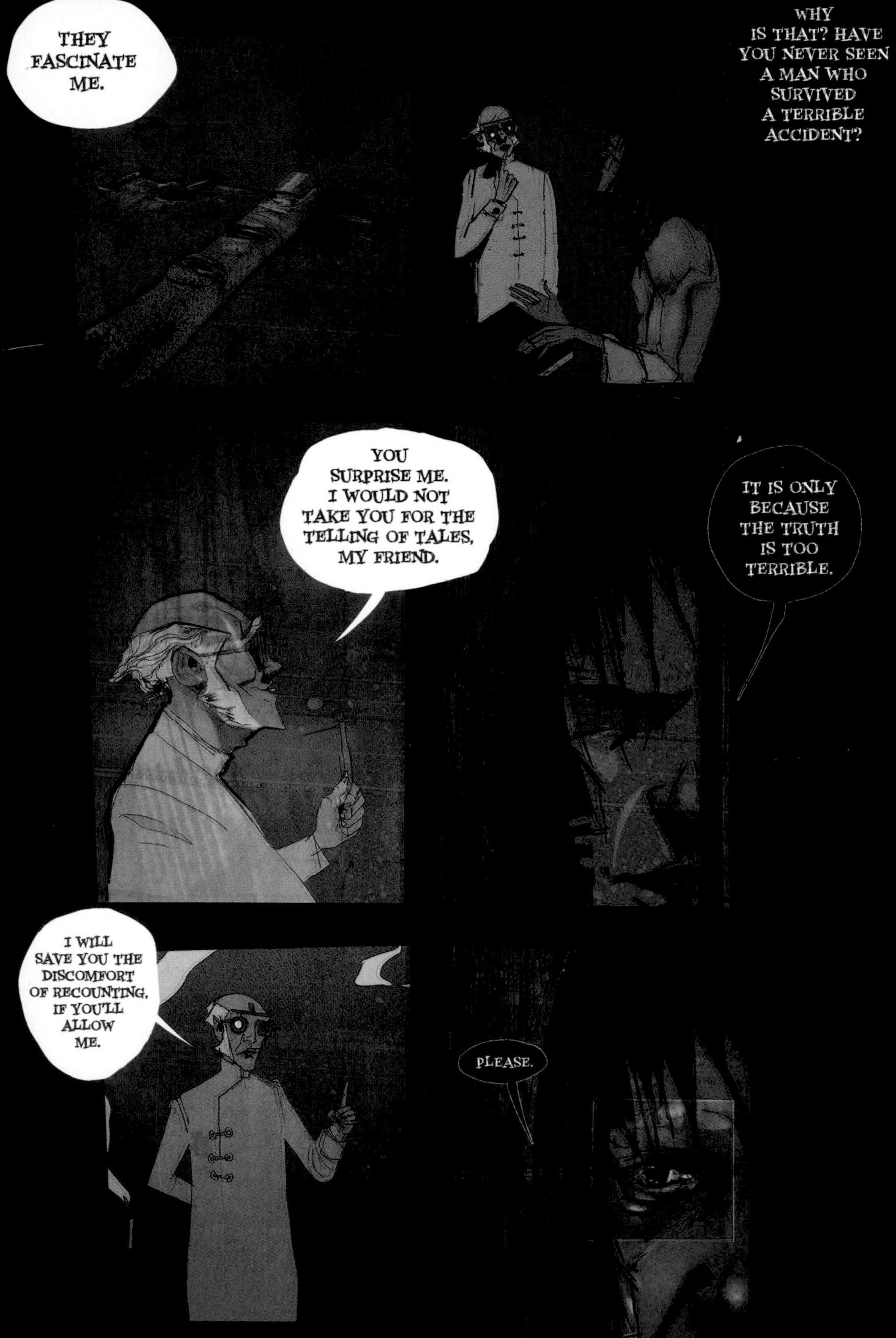
THEY FASCINATE ME.
WHY IS THAT? HAVE YOU NEVER SEEN A MAN WHO SURVIVED A TERRIBLE ACCIDENT?
YOU SURPRISE ME. I WOULD NOT TAKE YOU FOR THE TELLING OF TALES, MY FRIEND.
IT IS ONLY BECAUSE THE TRUTH IS TOO TERRIBLE.
I WILL SAVE YOU THE DISCOMFORT OF RECOUNTING, IF YOU'LL ALLOW ME.
PLEASE.

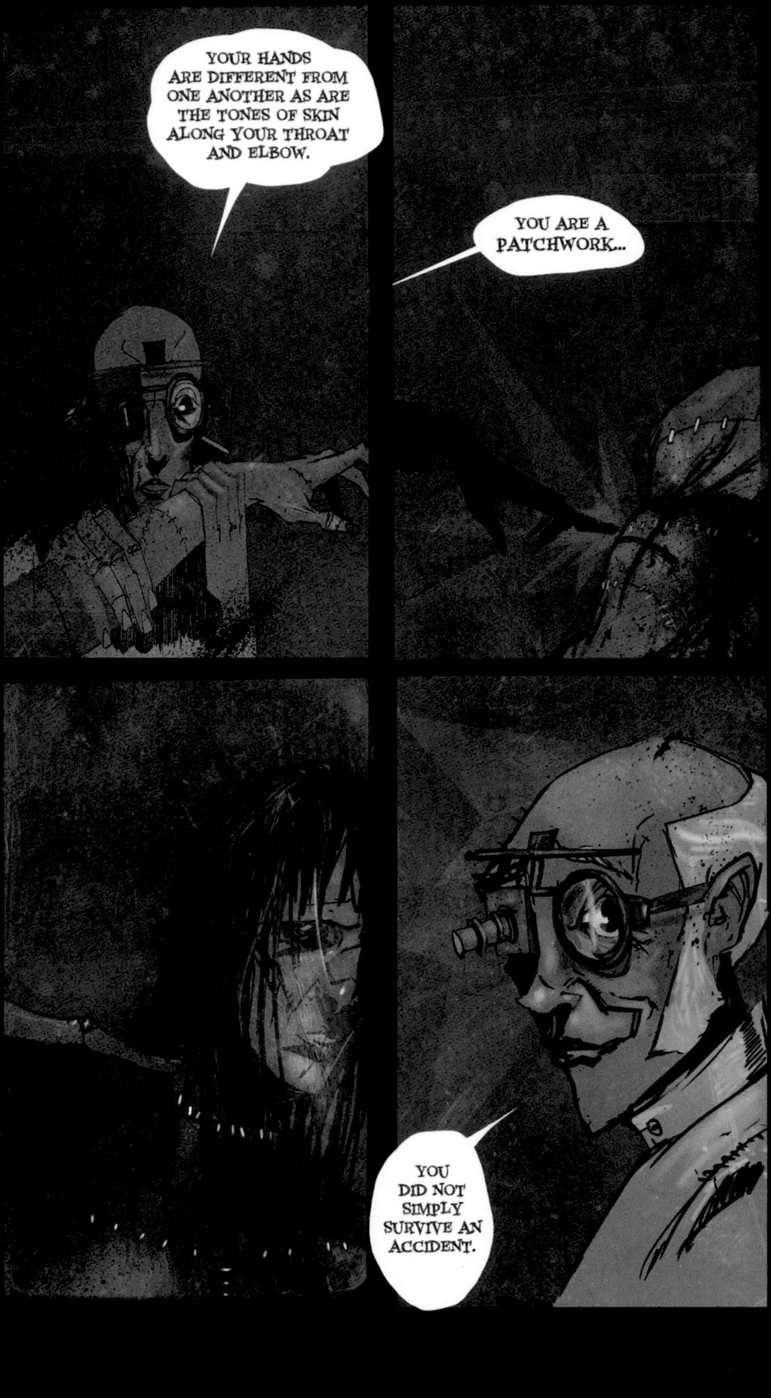

YOUR HANDS ARE DIFFERENT FROM ONE ANOTHER AS ARE THE TONES OF SKIN ALONG YOUR THROAT AND ELBOW.
YOU ARE A PATCHWORK...
YOU DID NOT SIMPLY SURVIVE AN ACCIDENT.

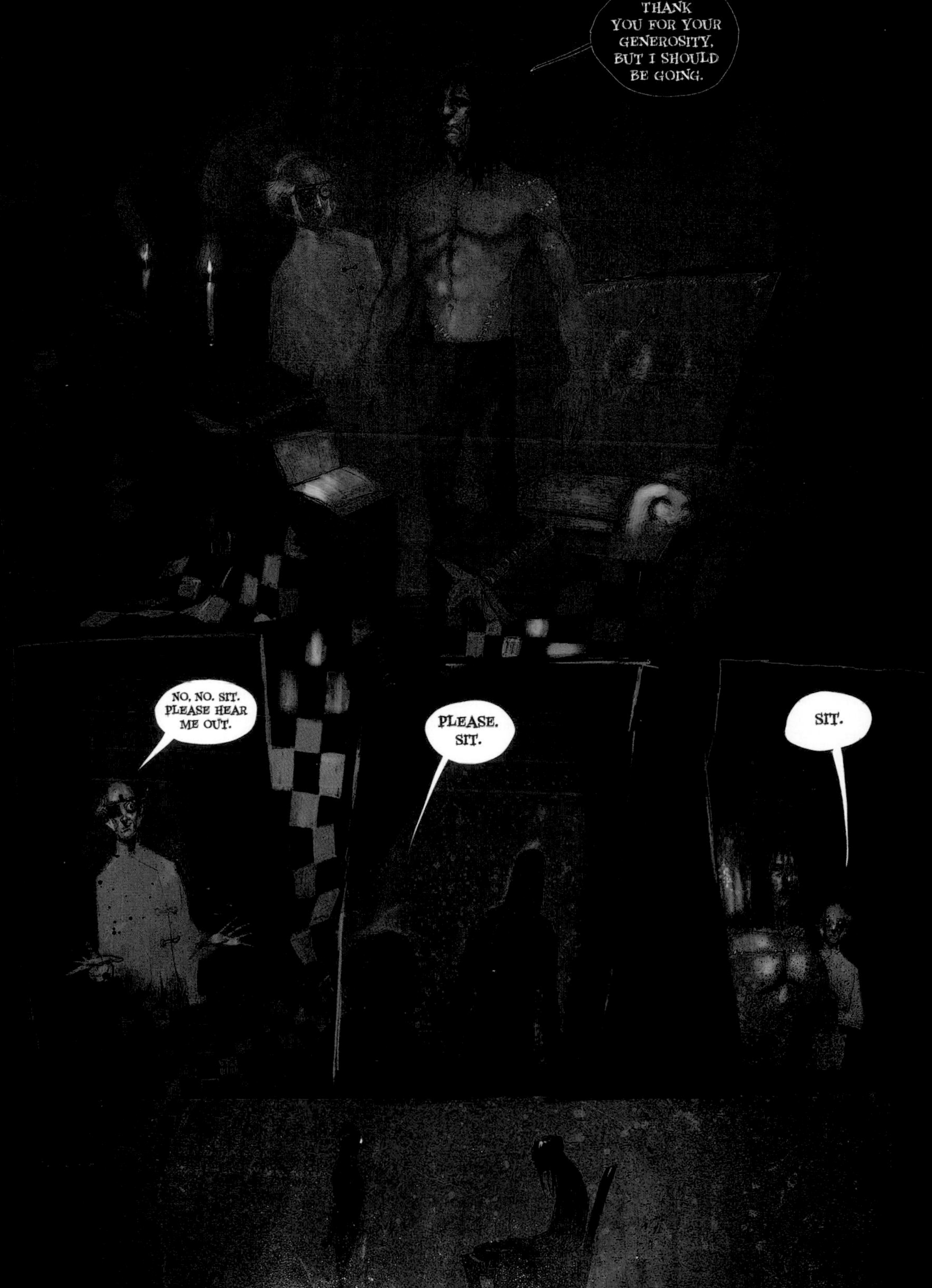
THANK YOU FOR YOUR GENEROSITY, BUT I SHOULD BE GOING.
NO, NO. SIT. PLEASE HEAR ME OUT.
PLEASE. SIT.
SIT.

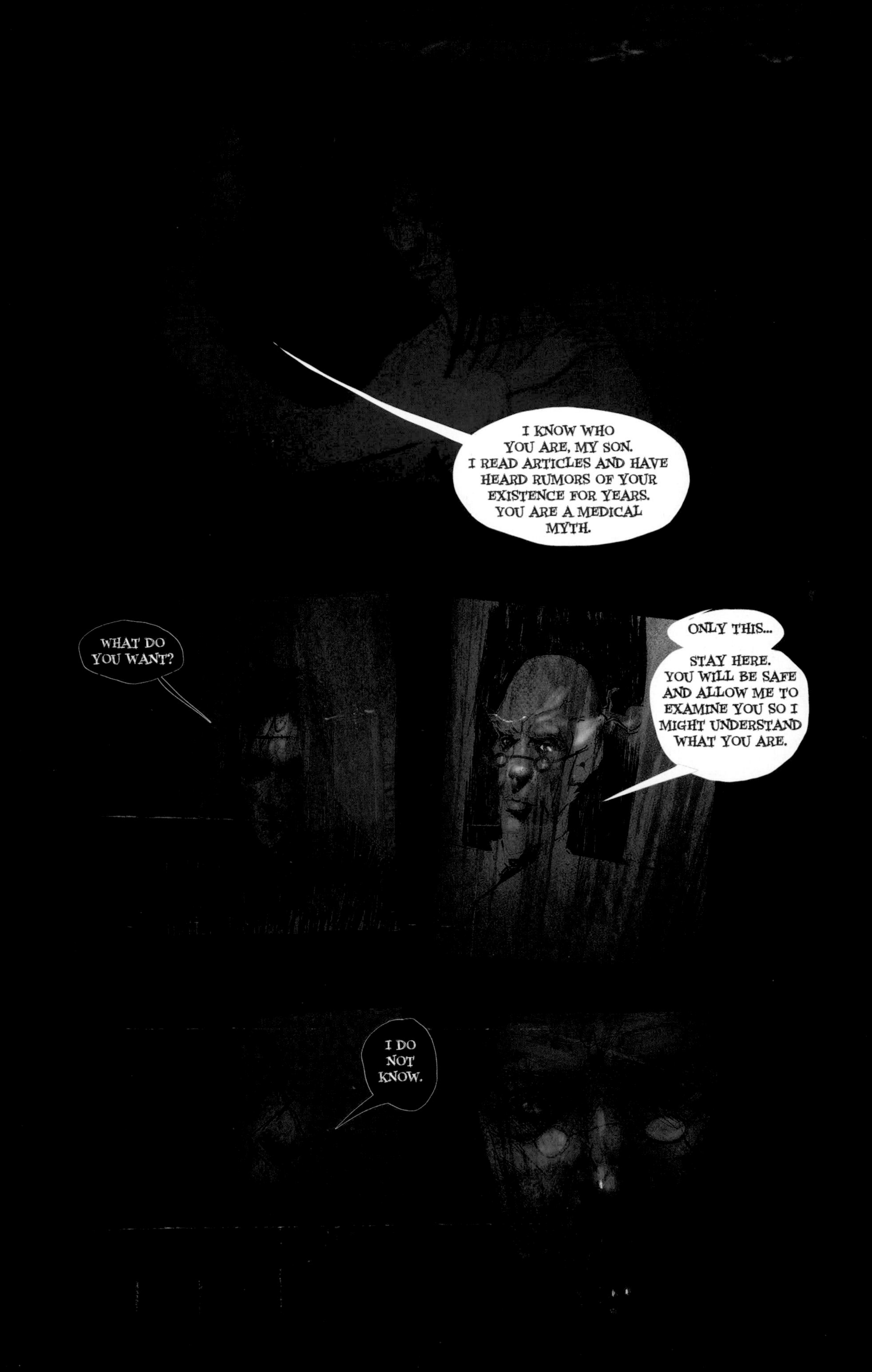
I KNOW WHO YOU ARE, MY SON. I READ ARTICLES AND HAVE HEARD RUMORS OF YOUR EXISTENCE FOR YEARS. YOU ARE A MEDICAL MYTH.
WHAT DO YOU WANT?
ONLY THIS...
STAY HERE. YOU WILL BE SAFE AND ALLOW ME TO EXAMINE YOU SO I MIGHT UNDERSTAND WHAT YOU ARE.
I DO NOT KNOW.

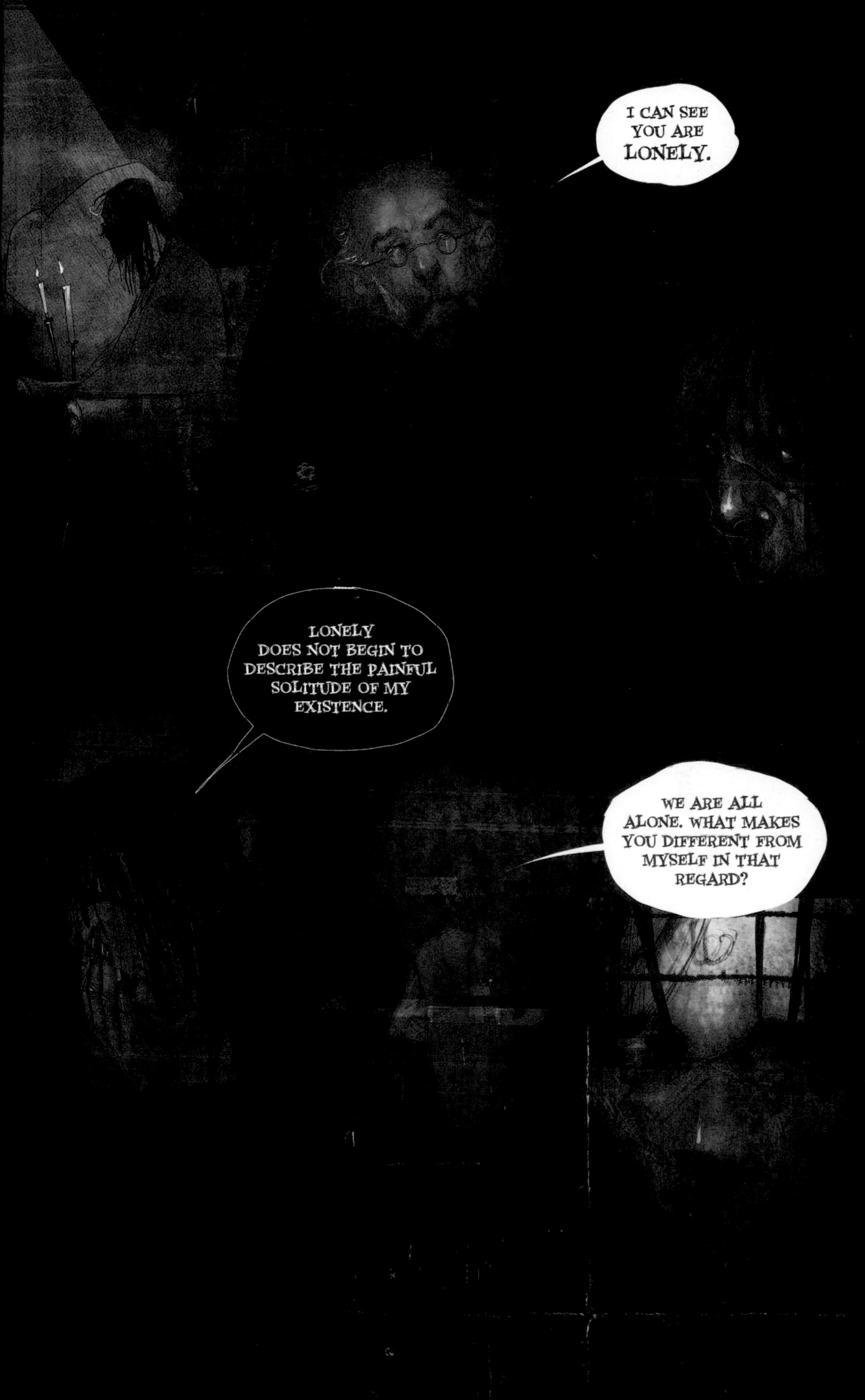
I CAN SEE YOU ARE LONELY.
LONELY DOES NOT BEGIN TO DESCRIBE THE PAINFUL SOLITUDE OF MY EXISTENCE.
WE ARE ALL ALONE. WHAT MAKES YOU DIFFERENT FROM MYSELF IN THAT REGARD?

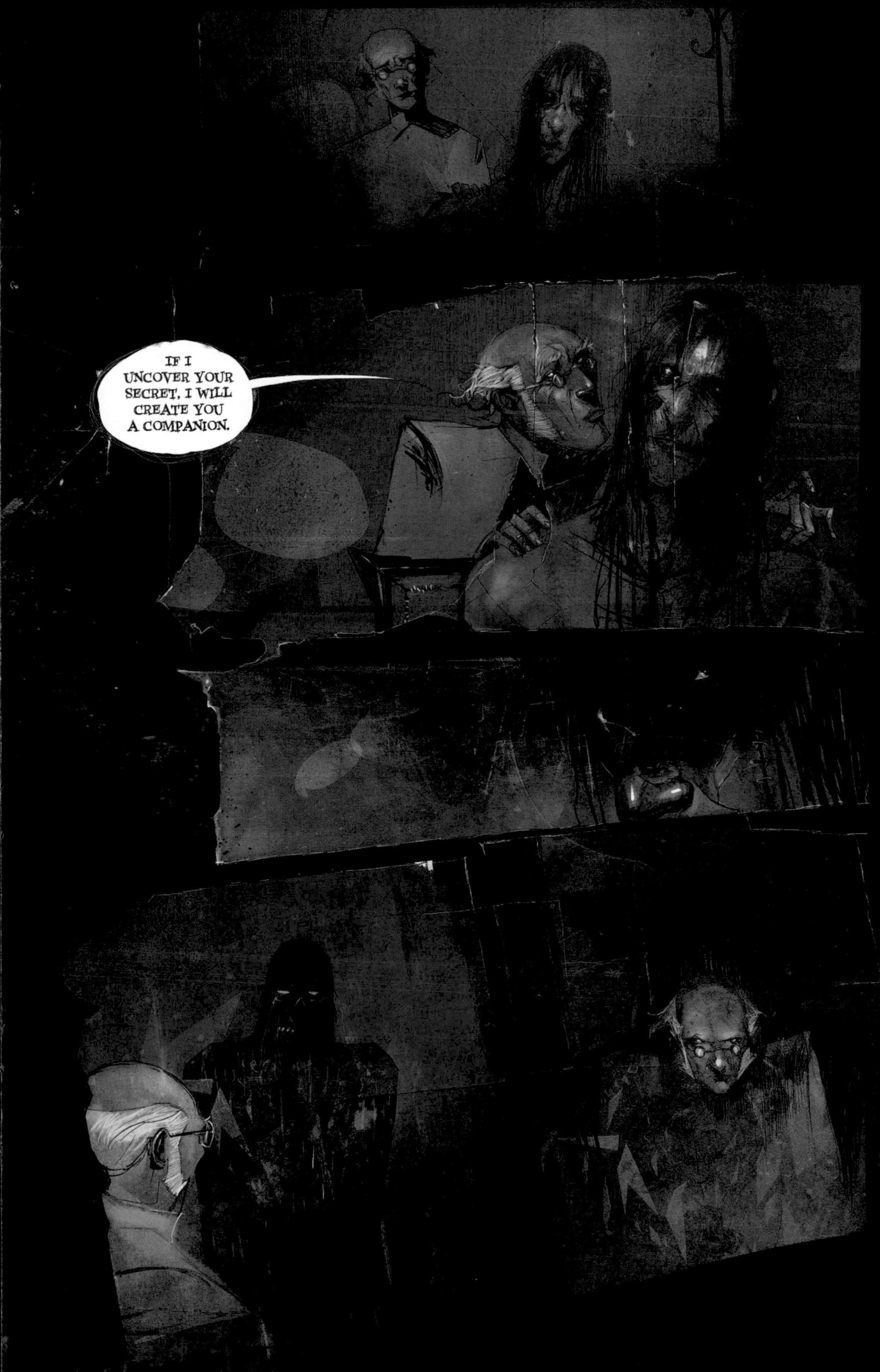
IF I UNCOVER YOUR SECRET, I WILL CREATE YOU A COMPANION.

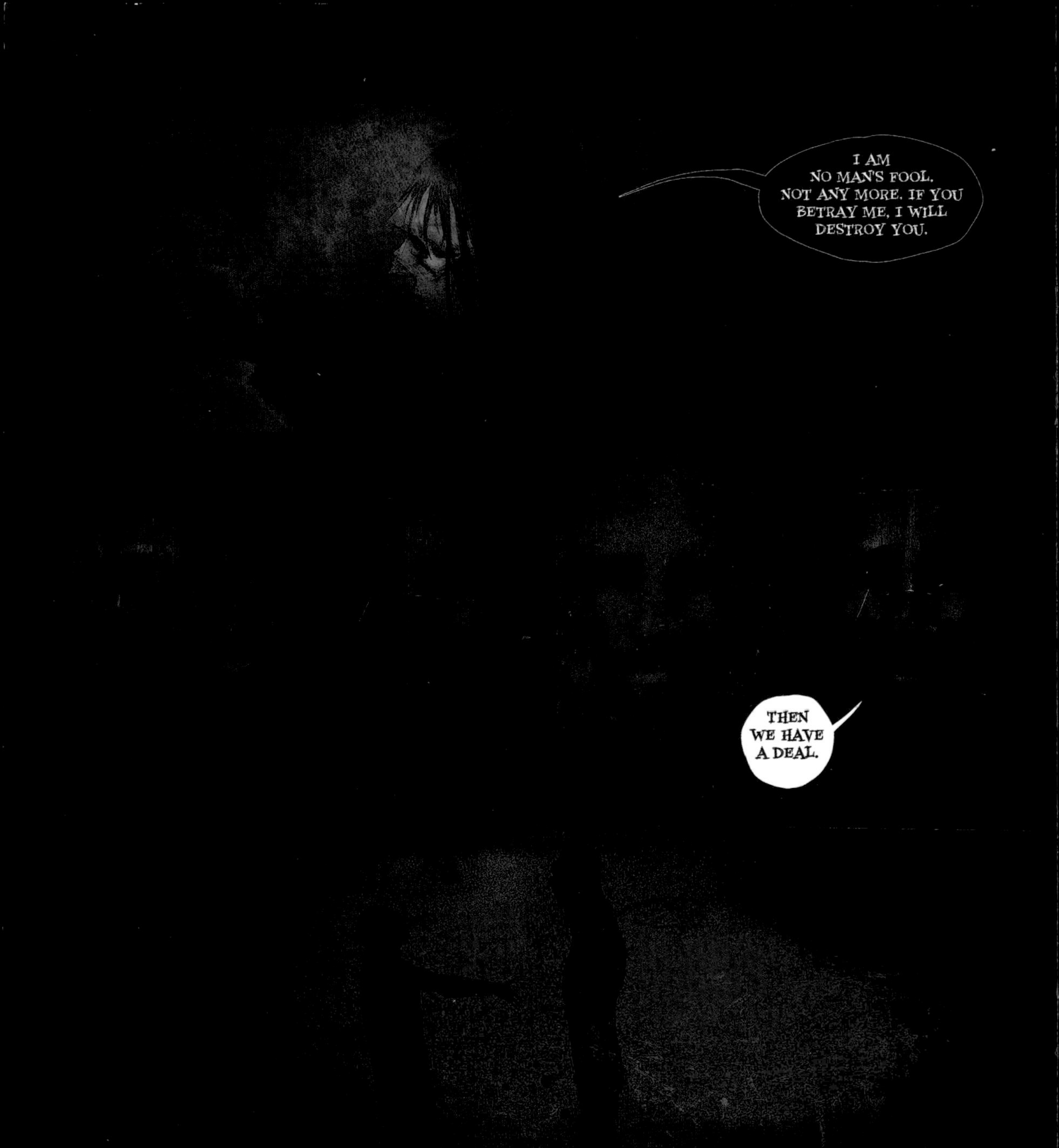
I AM NO MAN'S FOOL. NOT ANY MORE. IF YOU BETRAY ME, I WILL DESTROY YOU.
THEN WE HAVE A DEAL.

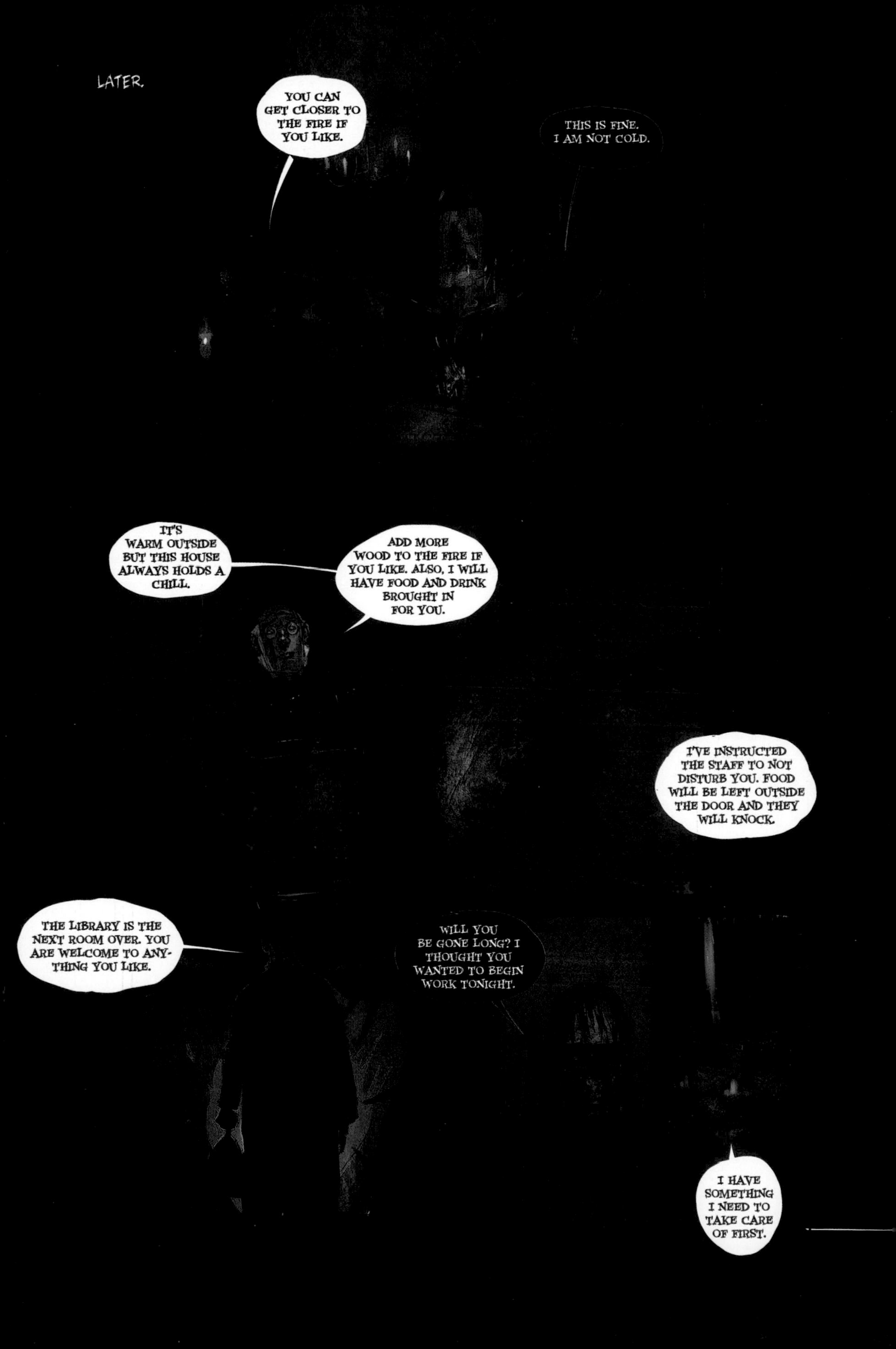
LATER.
YOU CAN GET CLOSER TO THE FIRE IF YOU LIKE.
THIS IS FINE. I AM NOT COLD.
IT'S WARM OUTSIDE BUT THIS HOUSE ALWAYS HOLDS A CHILL.
ADD MORE WOOD TO THE FIRE IF YOU LIKE. ALSO, I WILL HAVE FOOD AND DRINK BROUGHT IN FOR YOU.
I'VE INSTRUCTED THE STAFF TO NOT DISTURB YOU. FOOD WILL BE LEFT OUTSIDE THE DOOR AND THEY WILL KNOCK.
THE LIBRARY IS THE NEXT ROOM OVER. YOU ARE WELCOME TO ANY-THING YOU LIKE.
WILL YOU BE GONE LONG? I THOUGHT YOU WANTED TO BEGIN WORK TONIGHT.
I HAVE SOMETHING I NEED TO TAKE CARE OF FIRST.

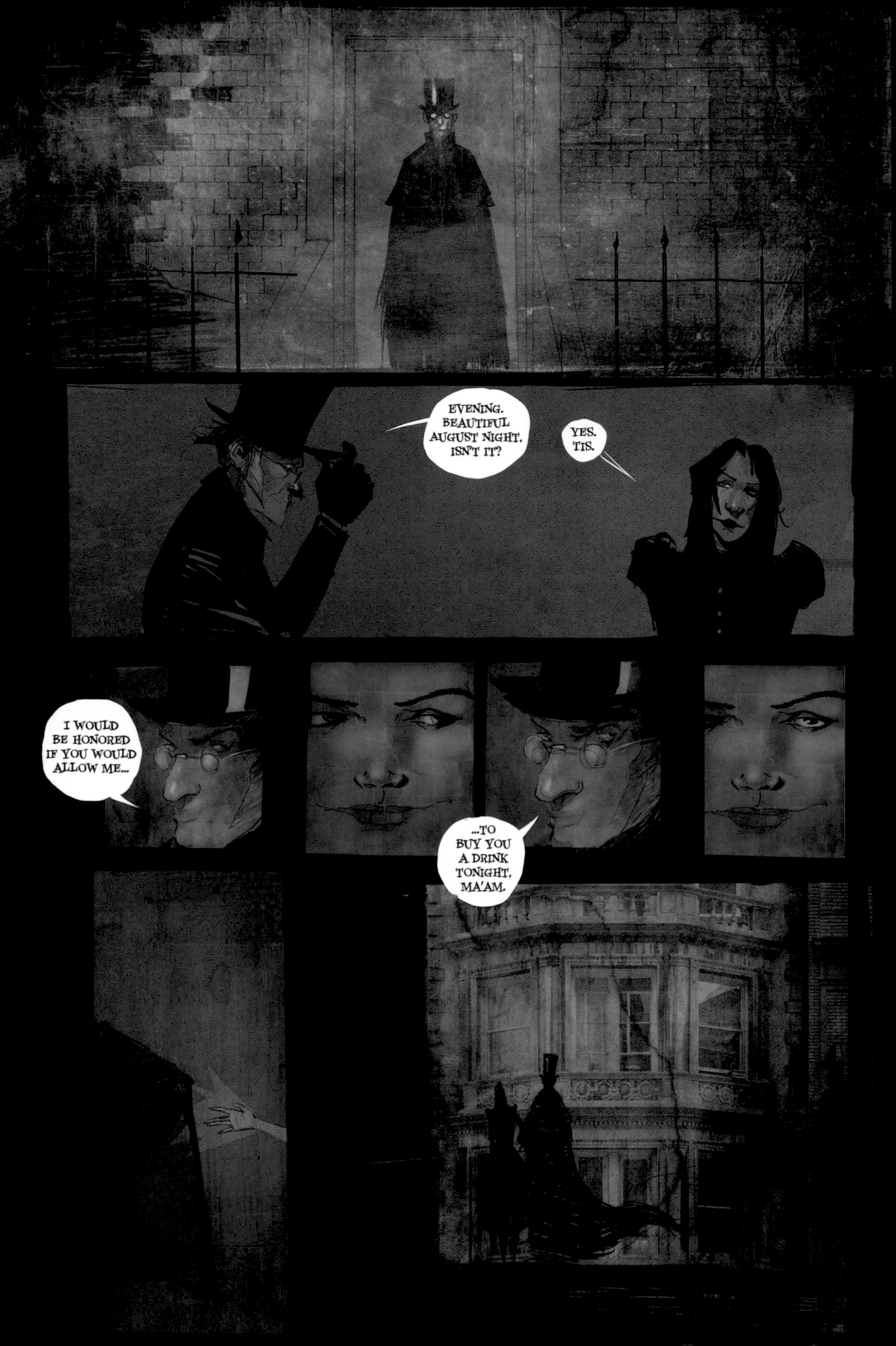
EVENING. BEAUTIFUL AUGUST NIGHT, ISN'T IT?
YES. TIS.
I WOULD BE HONORED IF YOU WOULD ALLOW ME...
...TO BUY YOU A DRINK TONIGHT, MA'AM.

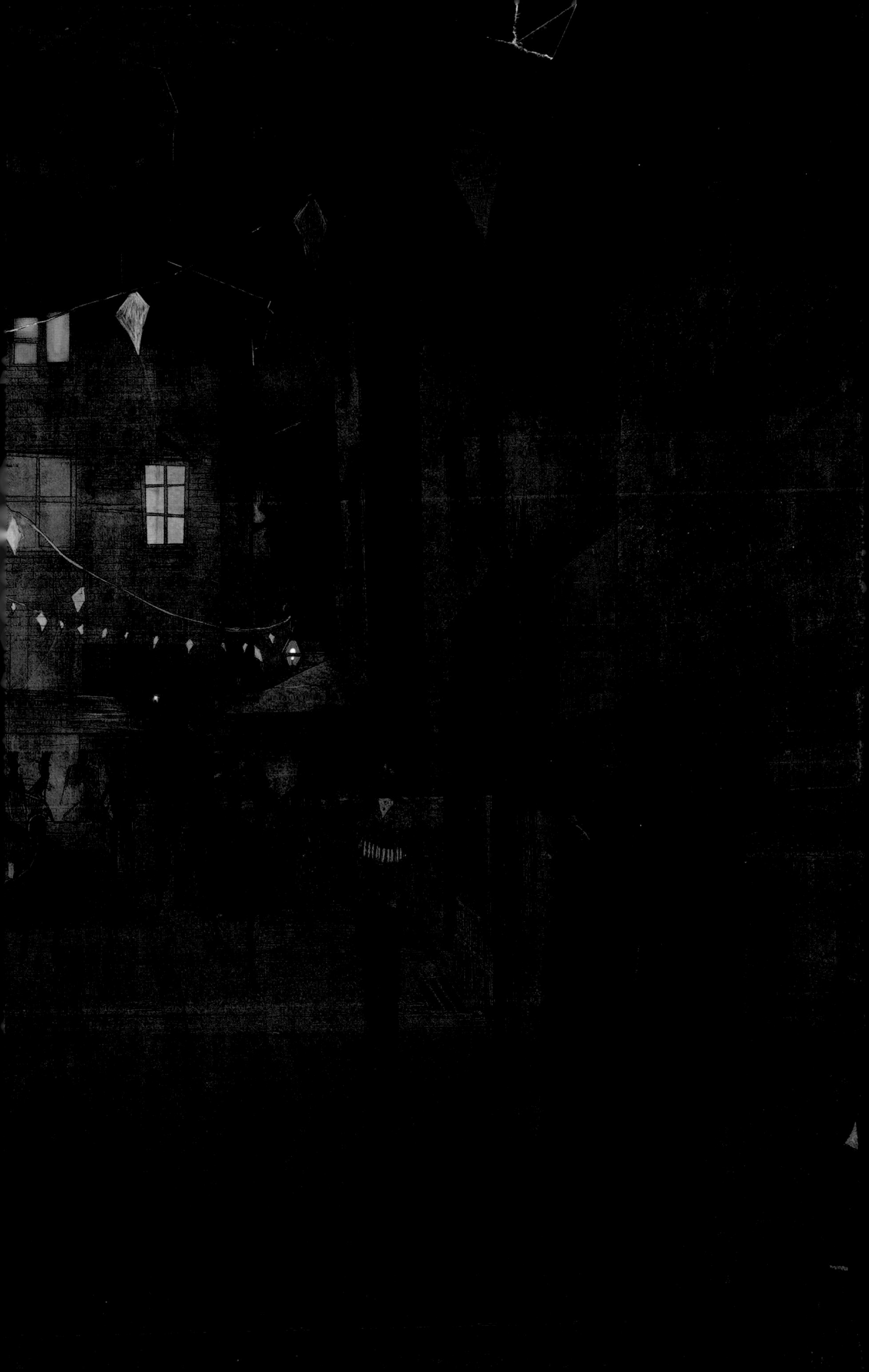

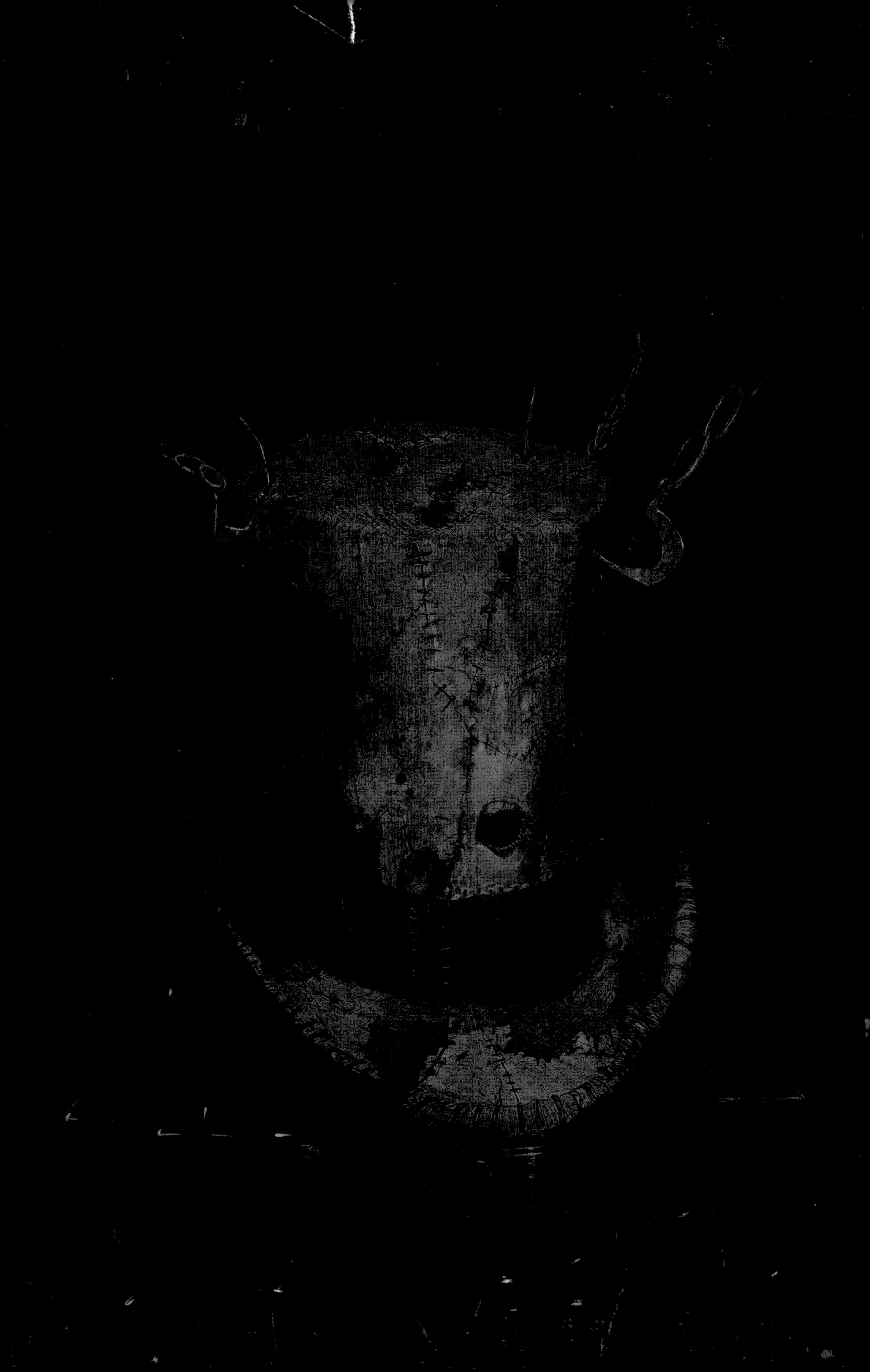

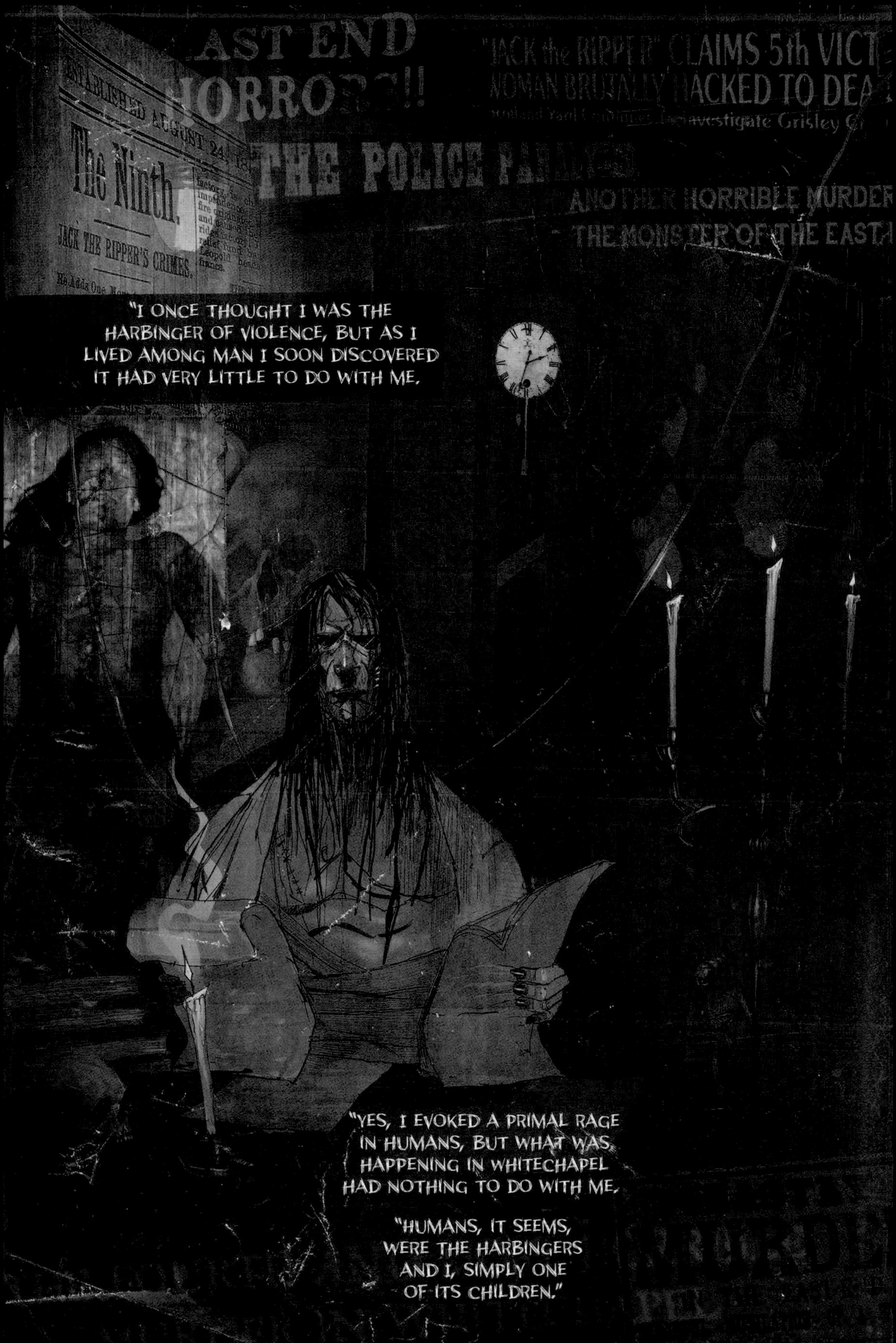
The Ninth.
JACK THE RIPPER'S CRIMES.
ANOTHER HORRIBLE MURDER
"I ONCE THOUGHT I WAS THE HARBINGER OF VIOLENCE, BUT AS I LIVED AMONG MAN I SOON DISCOVERED IT HAD VERY LITTLE TO DO WITH ME.
"YES, I EVOKED A PRIMAL RAGE IN HUMANS, BUT WHAT WAS HAPPENING IN WHITECHAPEL HAD NOTHING TO DO WITH ME.
"HUMANS, IT SEEMS, WERE THE HARBINGERS AND I, SIMPLY ONE OF ITS CHILDREN."

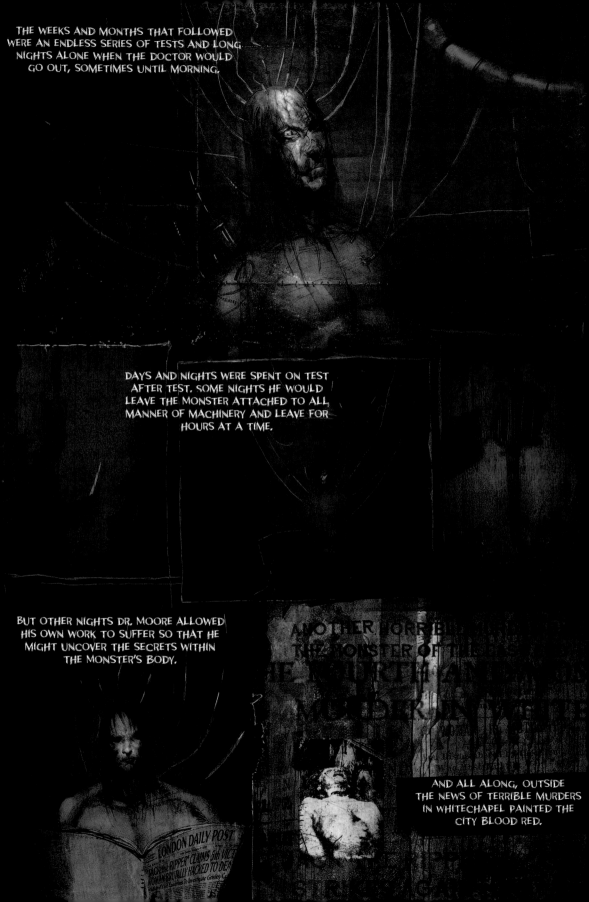

THE WEEKS AND MONTHS THAT FOLLOWED WERE AN ENDLESS SERIES OF TESTS AND LONG NIGHTS ALONE WHEN THE DOCTOR WOULD GO OUT, SOMETIMES UNTIL MORNING.

DAYS AND NIGHTS WERE SPENT ON TEST AFTER TEST. SOME NIGHTS HE WOULD LEAVE THE MONSTER ATTACHED TO ALL MANNER OF MACHINERY AND LEAVE FOR HOURS AT A TIME.

BUT OTHER NIGHTS DR. MOORE ALLOWED HIS OWN WORK TO SUFFER SO THAT HE MIGHT UNCOVER THE SECRETS WITHIN THE MONSTER'S BODY.

AND ALL ALONG, OUTSIDE THE NEWS OF TERRIBLE MURDERS IN WHITECHAPEL PAINTED THE CITY BLOOD RED.

LONDON DAILY POST

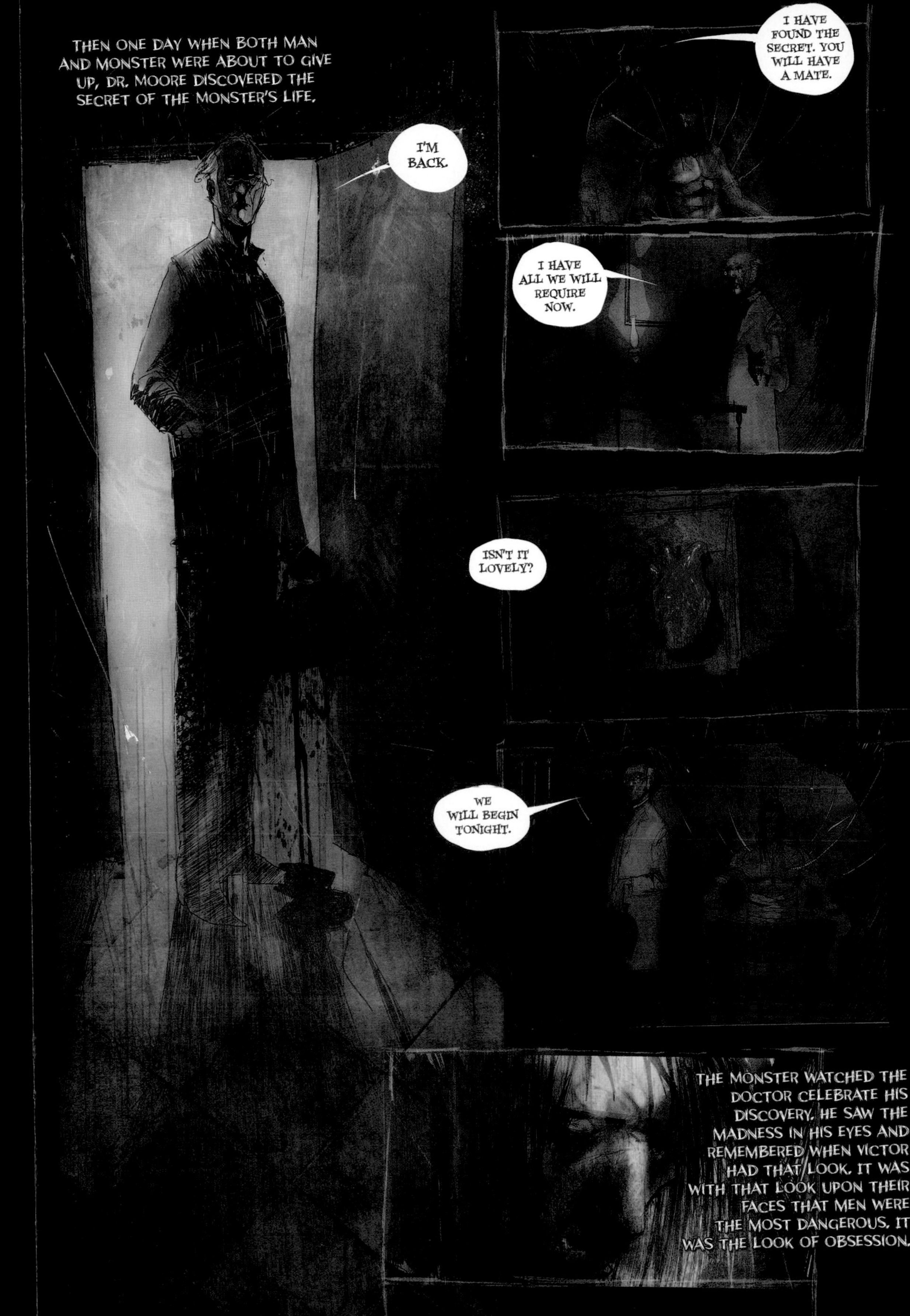
THEN ONE DAY WHEN BOTH MAN AND MONSTER WERE ABOUT TO GIVE UP, DR. MOORE DISCOVERED THE SECRET OF THE MONSTER'S LIFE.
I'M BACK.
I HAVE FOUND THE SECRET. YOU WILL HAVE A MATE.
I HAVE ALL WE WILL REQUIRE NOW.
ISN'T IT LOVELY?
WE WILL BEGIN TONIGHT.
THE MONSTER WATCHED THE DOCTOR CELEBRATE HIS DISCOVERY. HE SAW THE MADNESS IN HIS EYES AND REMEMBERED WHEN VICTOR HAD THAT LOOK. IT WAS WITH THAT LOOK UPON THEIR FACES THAT MEN WERE THE MOST DANGEROUS. IT WAS THE LOOK OF OBSESSION.

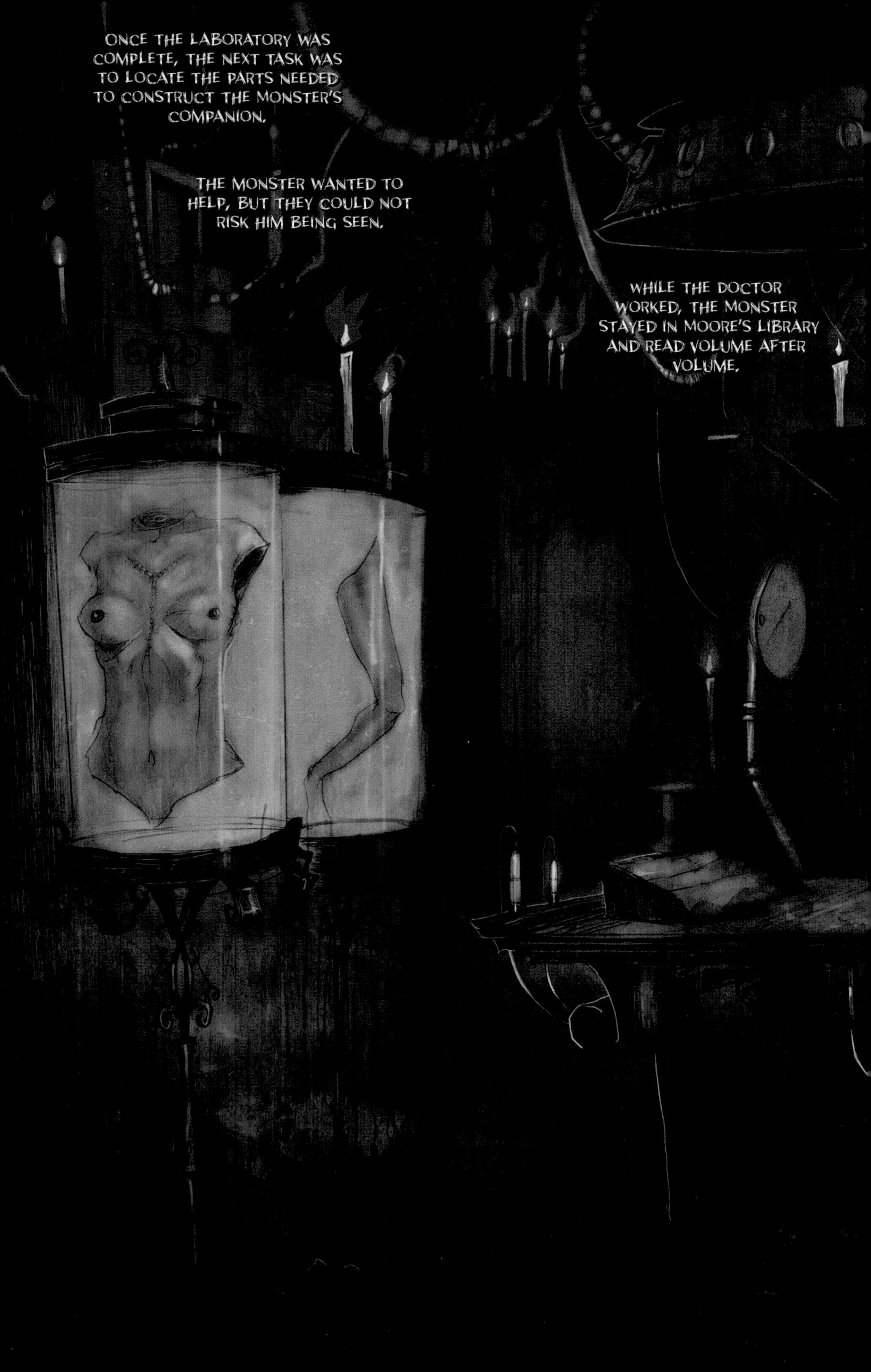
ONCE THE LABORATORY WAS COMPLETE, THE NEXT TASK WAS TO LOCATE THE PARTS NEEDED TO CONSTRUCT THE MONSTER'S COMPANION.
THE MONSTER WANTED TO HELP, BUT THEY COULD NOT RISK HIM BEING SEEN.
WHILE THE DOCTOR WORKED, THE MONSTER STAYED IN MOORE'S LIBRARY AND READ VOLUME AFTER VOLUME.

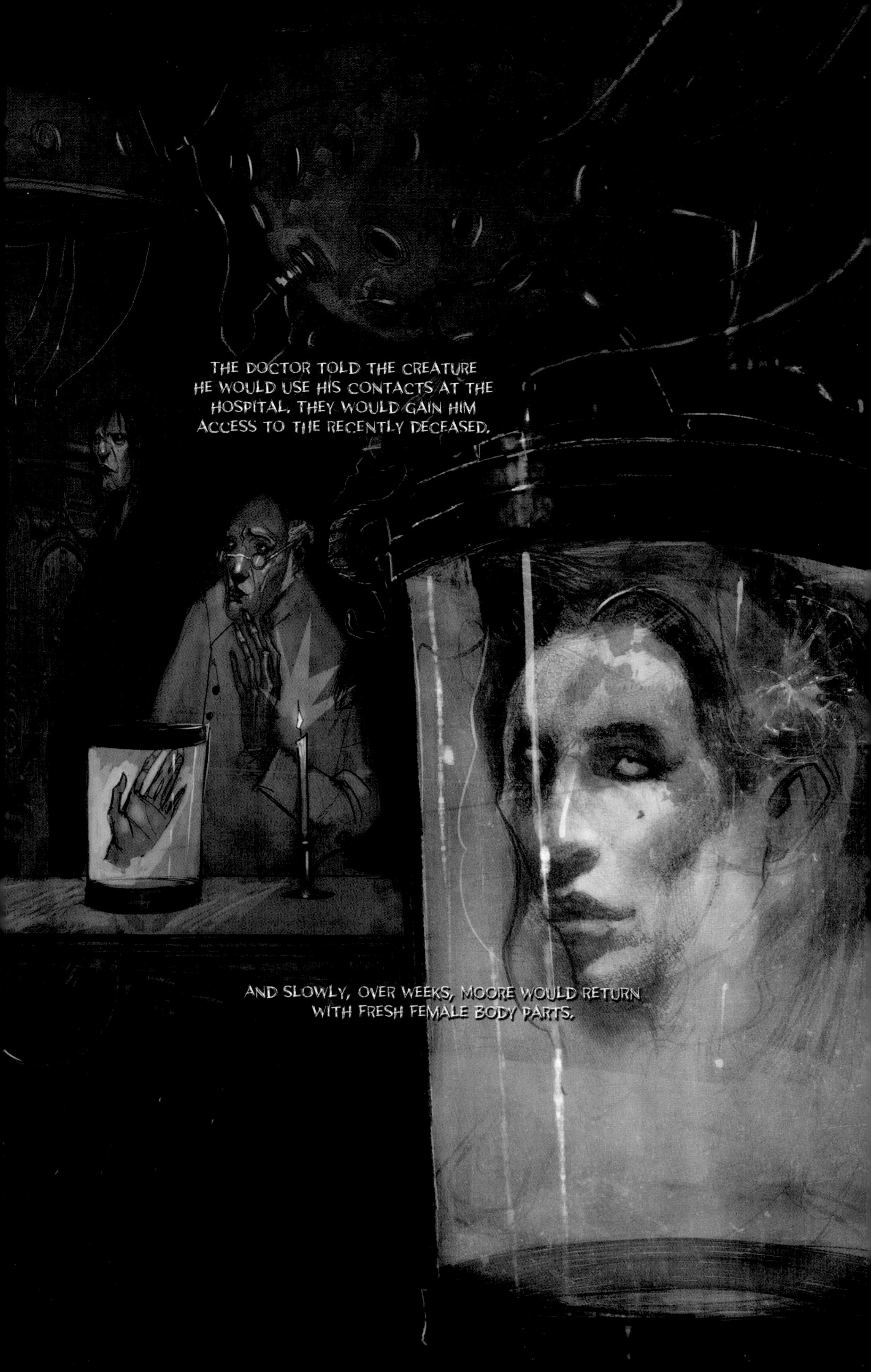
THE DOCTOR TOLD THE CREATURE HE WOULD USE HIS CONTACTS AT THE HOSPITAL. THEY WOULD GAIN HIM ACCESS TO THE RECENTLY DECEASED.
AND SLOWLY, OVER WEEKS, MOORE WOULD RETURN WITH FRESH FEMALE BODY PARTS.

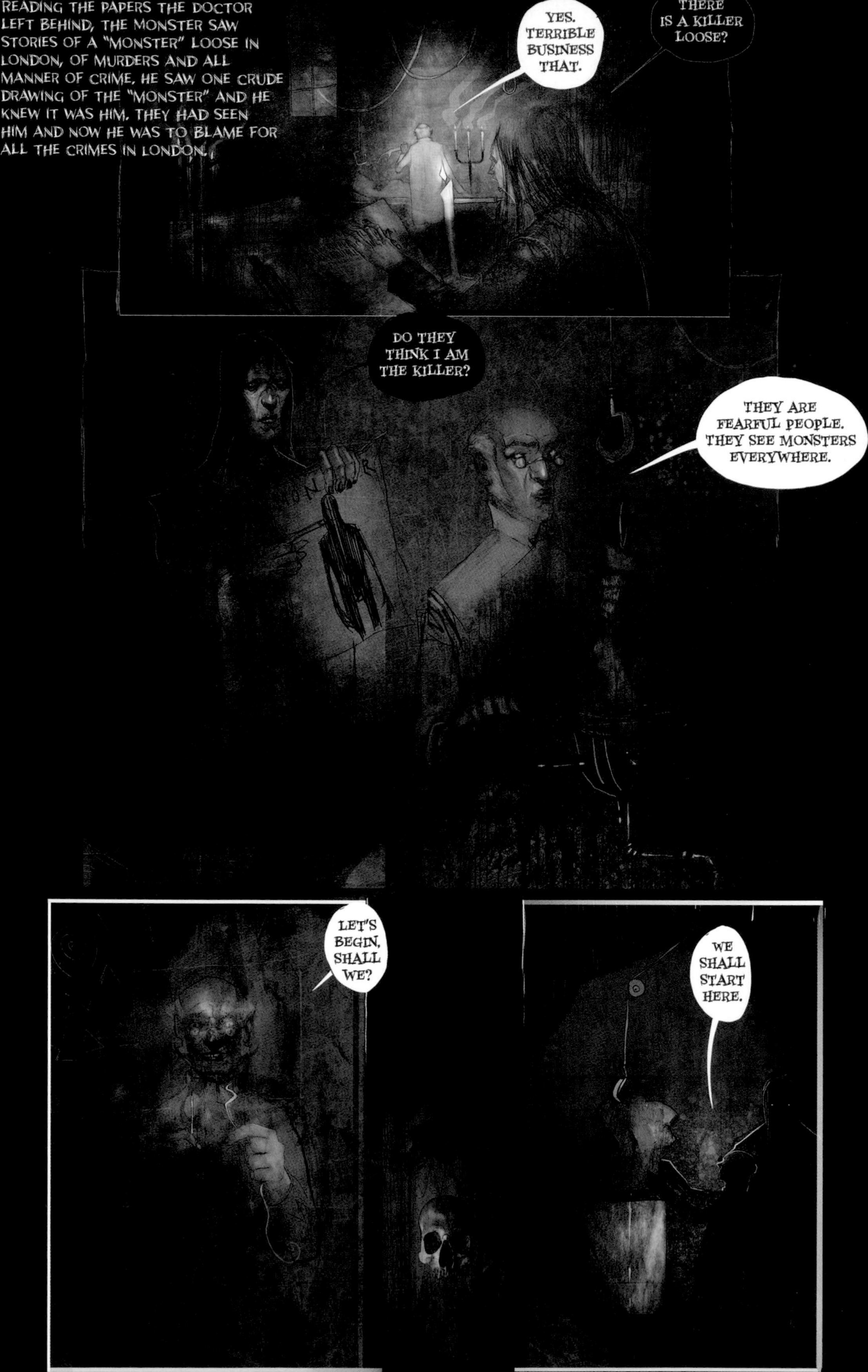

READING THE PAPERS THE DOCTOR LEFT BEHIND, THE MONSTER SAW STORIES OF A "MONSTER" LOOSE IN LONDON, OF MURDERS AND ALL MANNER OF CRIME. HE SAW ONE CRUDE DRAWING OF THE "MONSTER" AND HE KNEW IT WAS HIM. THEY HAD SEEN HIM AND NOW HE WAS TO BLAME FOR ALL THE CRIMES IN LONDON.
THERE IS A KILLER LOOSE?
YES. TERRIBLE BUSINESS THAT.
DO THEY THINK I AM THE KILLER?
THEY ARE FEARFUL PEOPLE. THEY SEE MONSTERS EVERYWHERE.
LET'S BEGIN, SHALL WE?
WE SHALL START HERE.

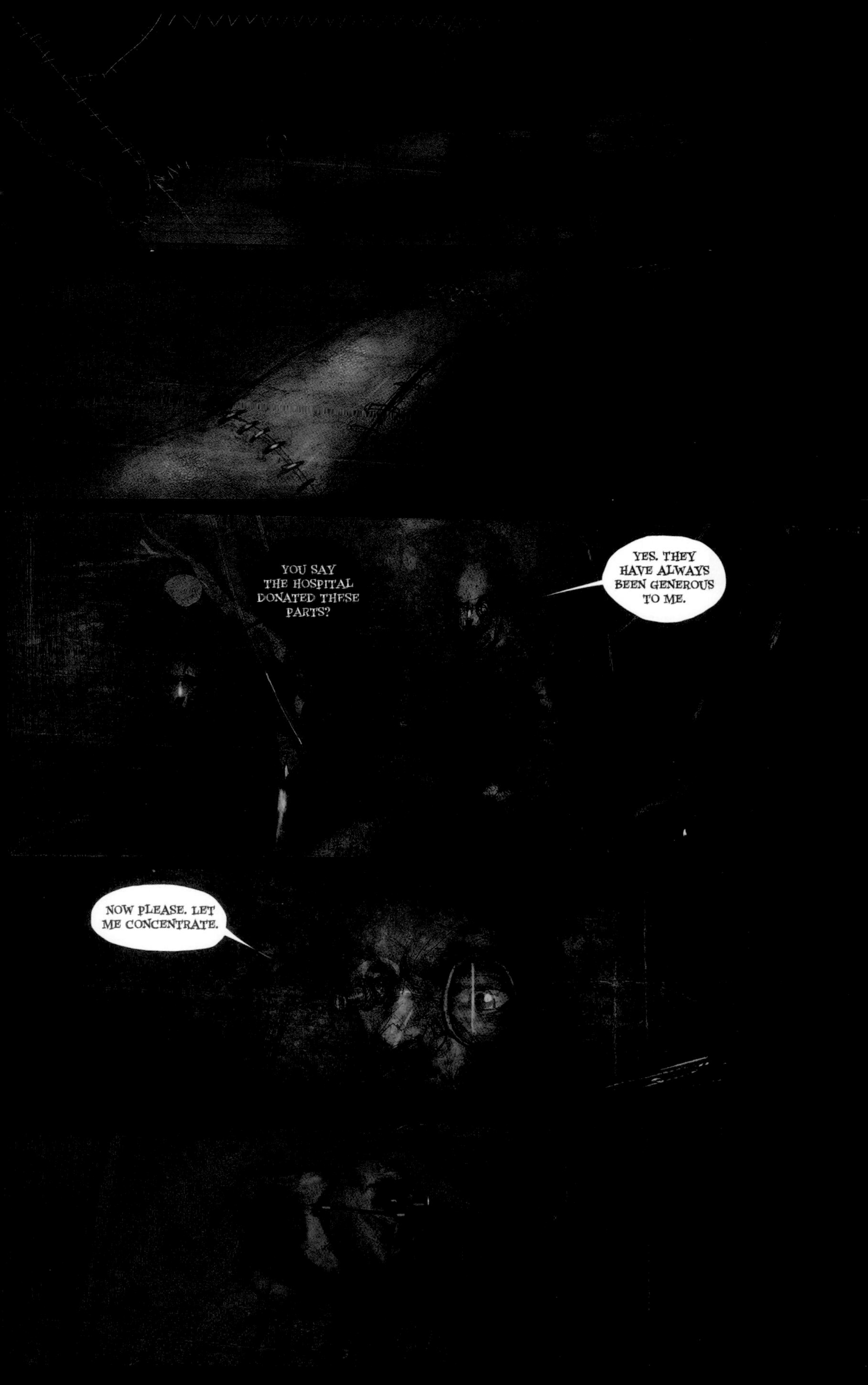
YOU SAY THE HOSPITAL DONATED THESE PARTS?
YES. THEY HAVE ALWAYS BEEN GENEROUS TO ME.
NOW PLEASE. LET ME CONCENTRATE.

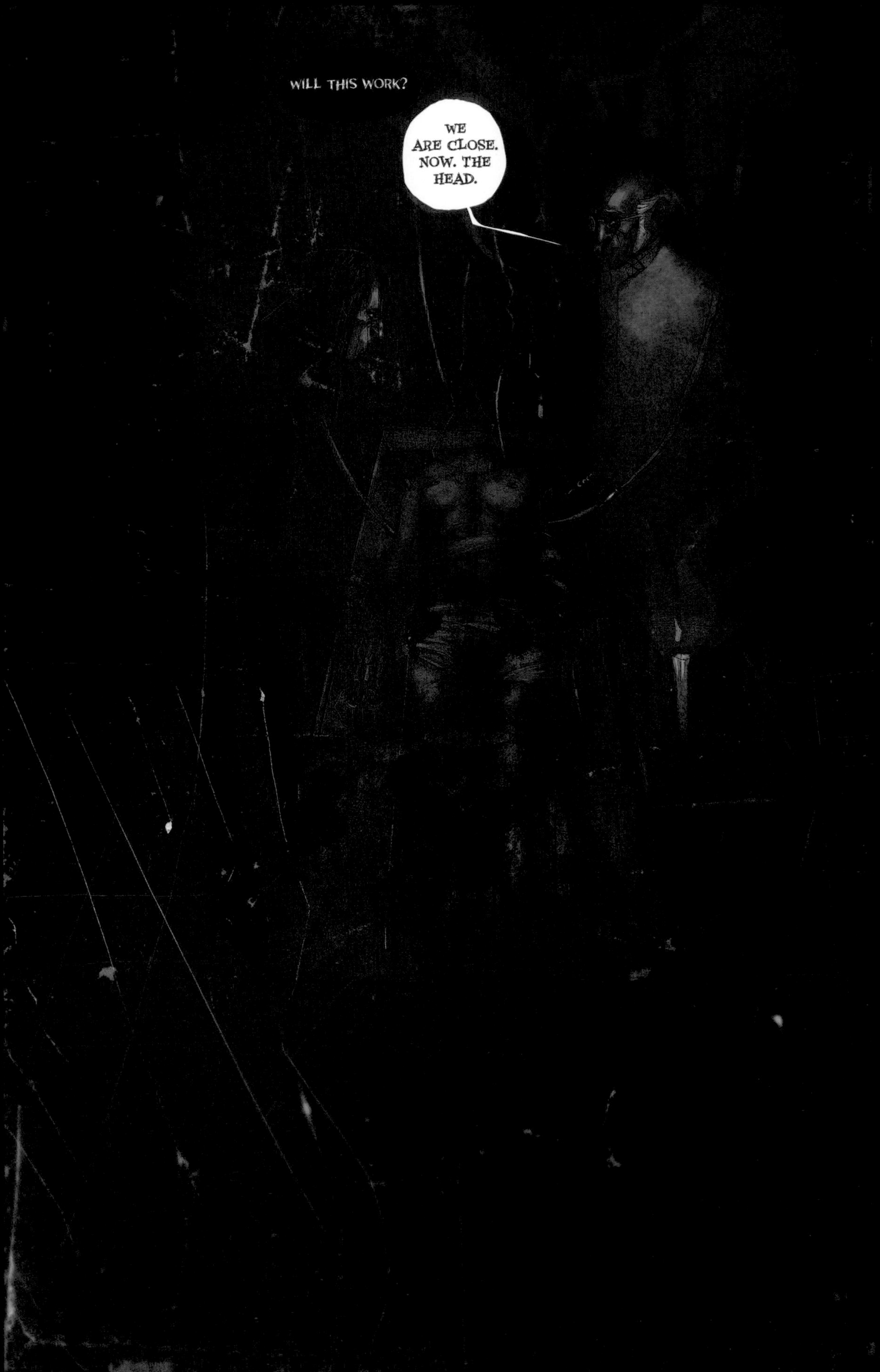
WILL THIS WORK?
WE ARE CLOSE. NOW. THE HEAD.

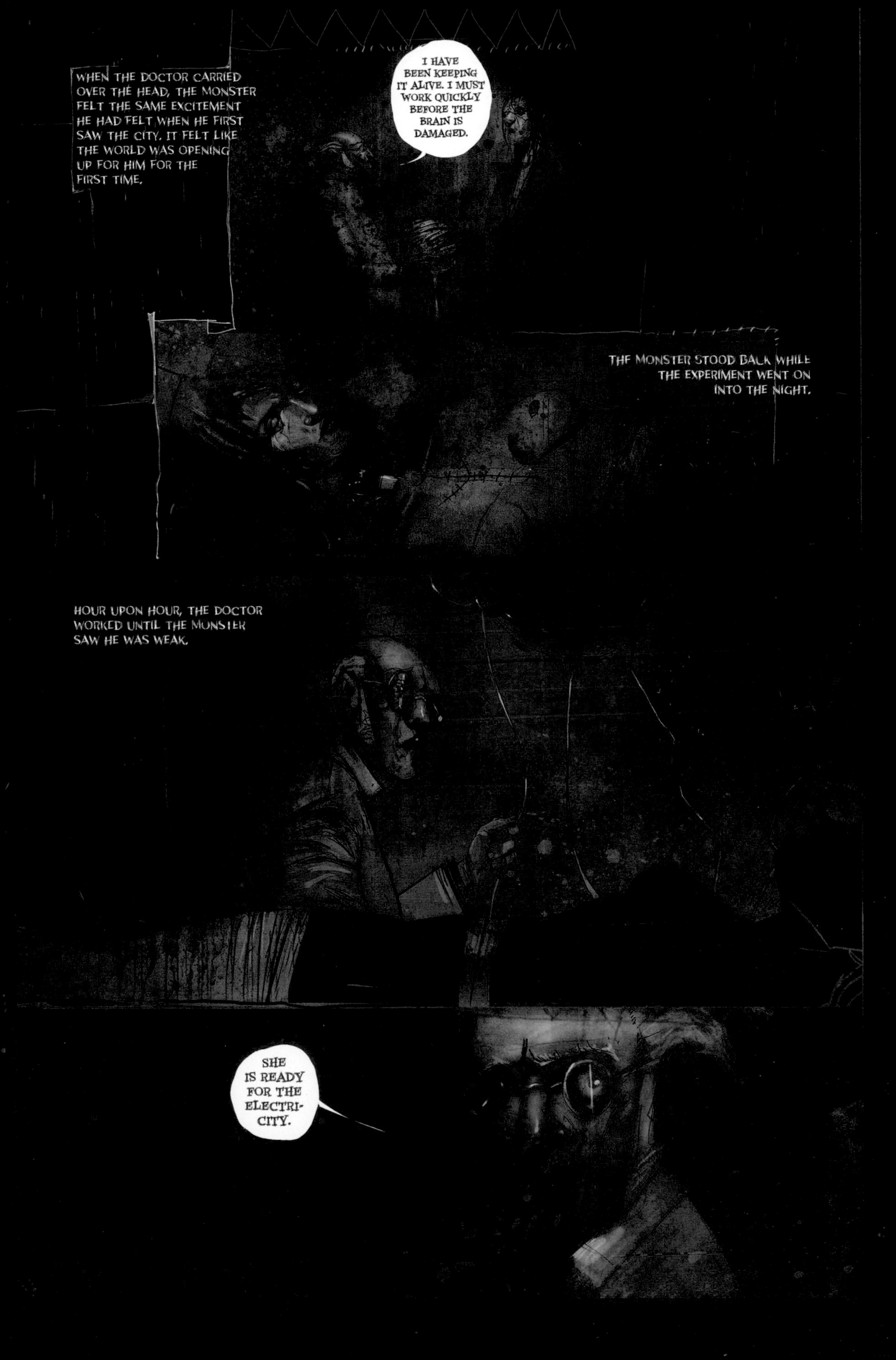
WHEN THE DOCTOR CARRIED OVER THE HEAD, THE MONSTER FELT THE SAME EXCITEMENT HE HAD FELT WHEN HE FIRST SAW THE CITY. IT FELT LIKE THE WORLD WAS OPENING UP FOR HIM FOR THE FIRST TIME.
I HAVE BEEN KEEPING IT ALIVE. I MUST WORK QUICKLY BEFORE THE BRAIN IS DAMAGED.
THE MONSTER STOOD BACK WHILE THE EXPERIMENT WENT ON INTO THE NIGHT.
HOUR UPON HOUR, THE DOCTOR WORKED UNTIL THE MONSTER SAW HE WAS WEAK.
SHE IS READY FOR THE ELECTRICITY.

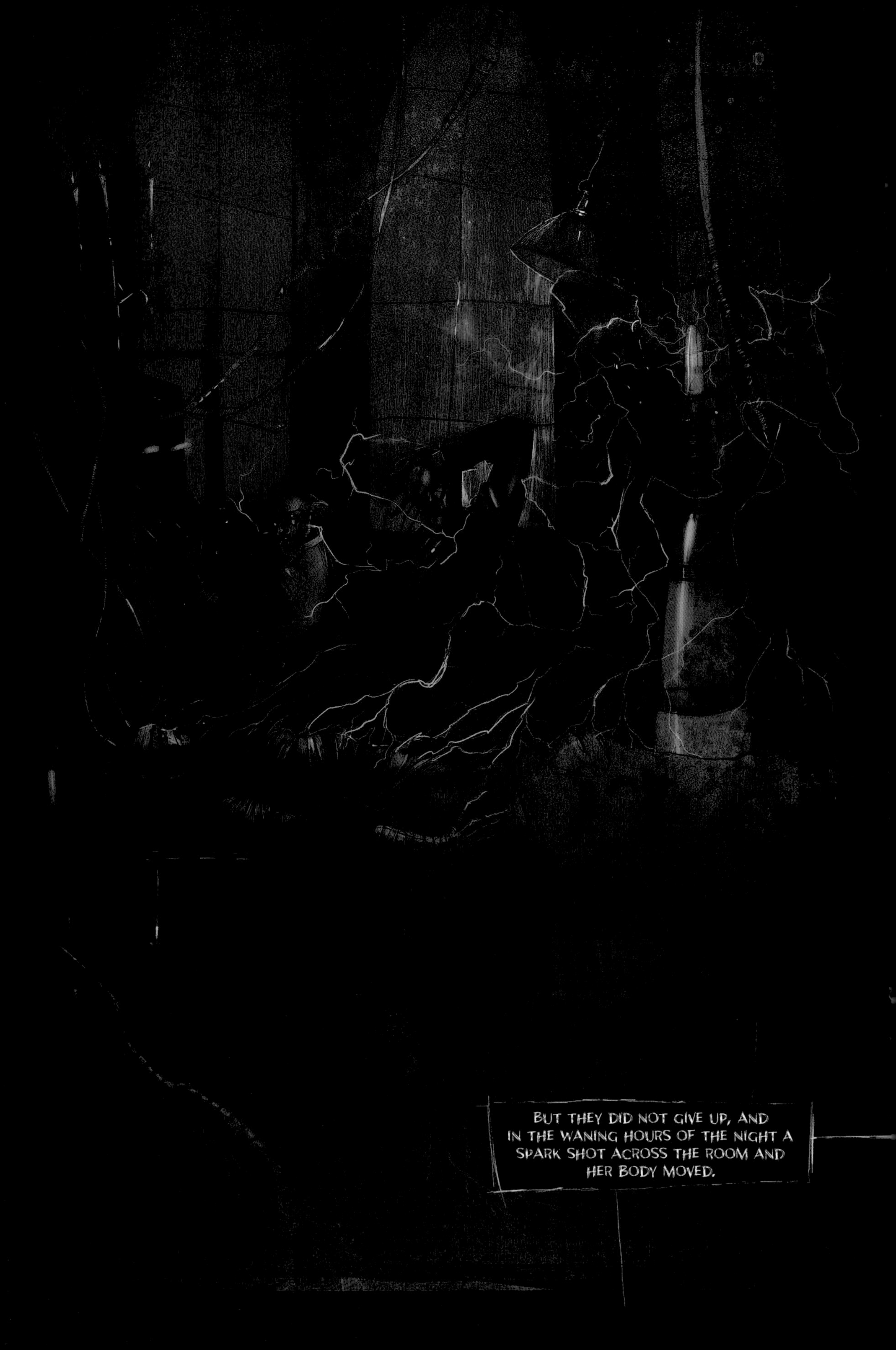
BUT THEY DID NOT GIVE UP, AND IN THE WANING HOURS OF THE NIGHT A SPARK SHOT ACROSS THE ROOM AND HER BODY MOVED.

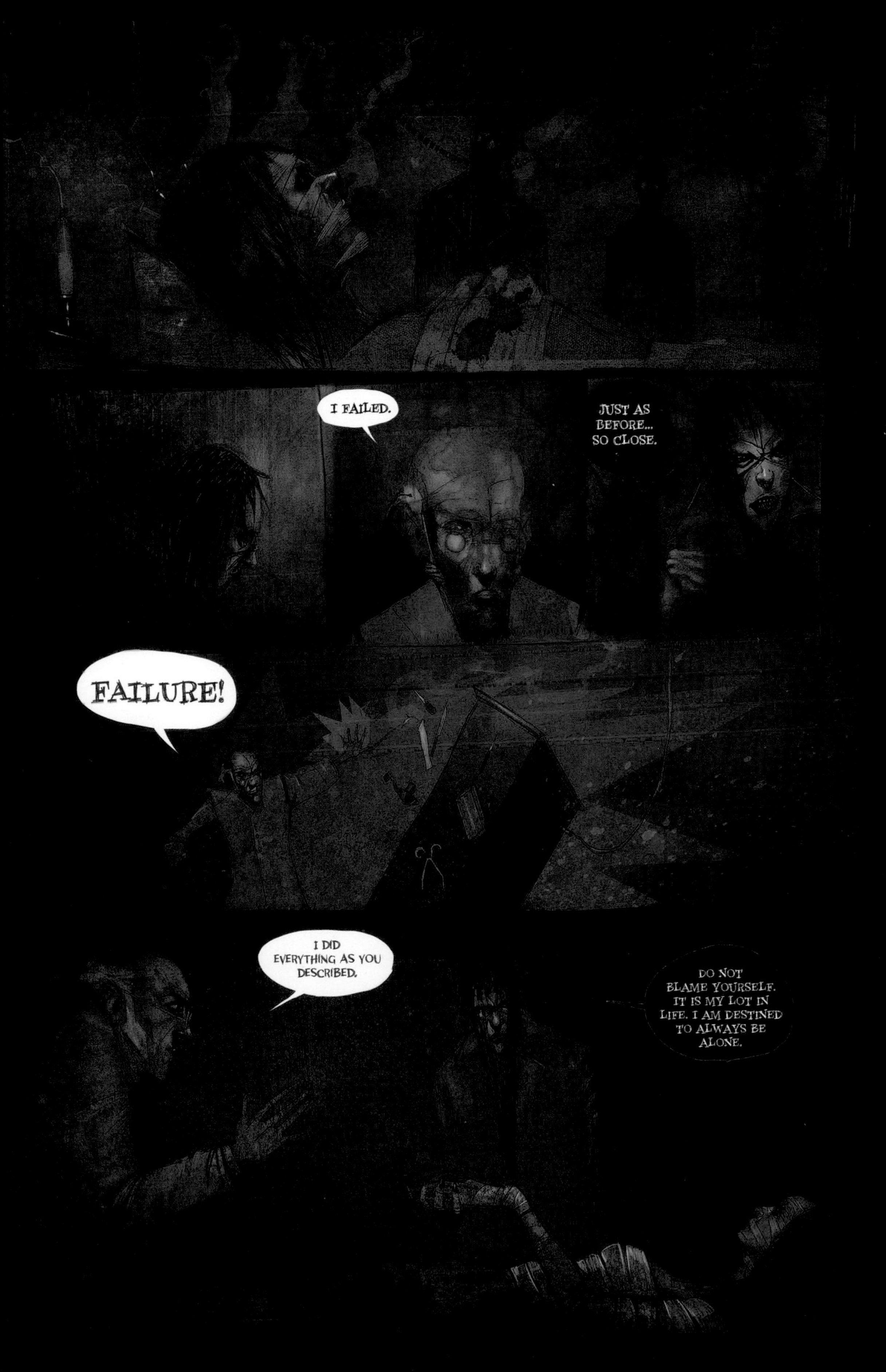
I FAILED.
JUST AS BEFORE... SO CLOSE.
FAILURE!
I DID EVERYTHING AS YOU DESCRIBED.
DO NOT BLAME YOURSELF. IT IS MY LOT IN LIFE. I AM DESTINED TO ALWAYS BE ALONE.

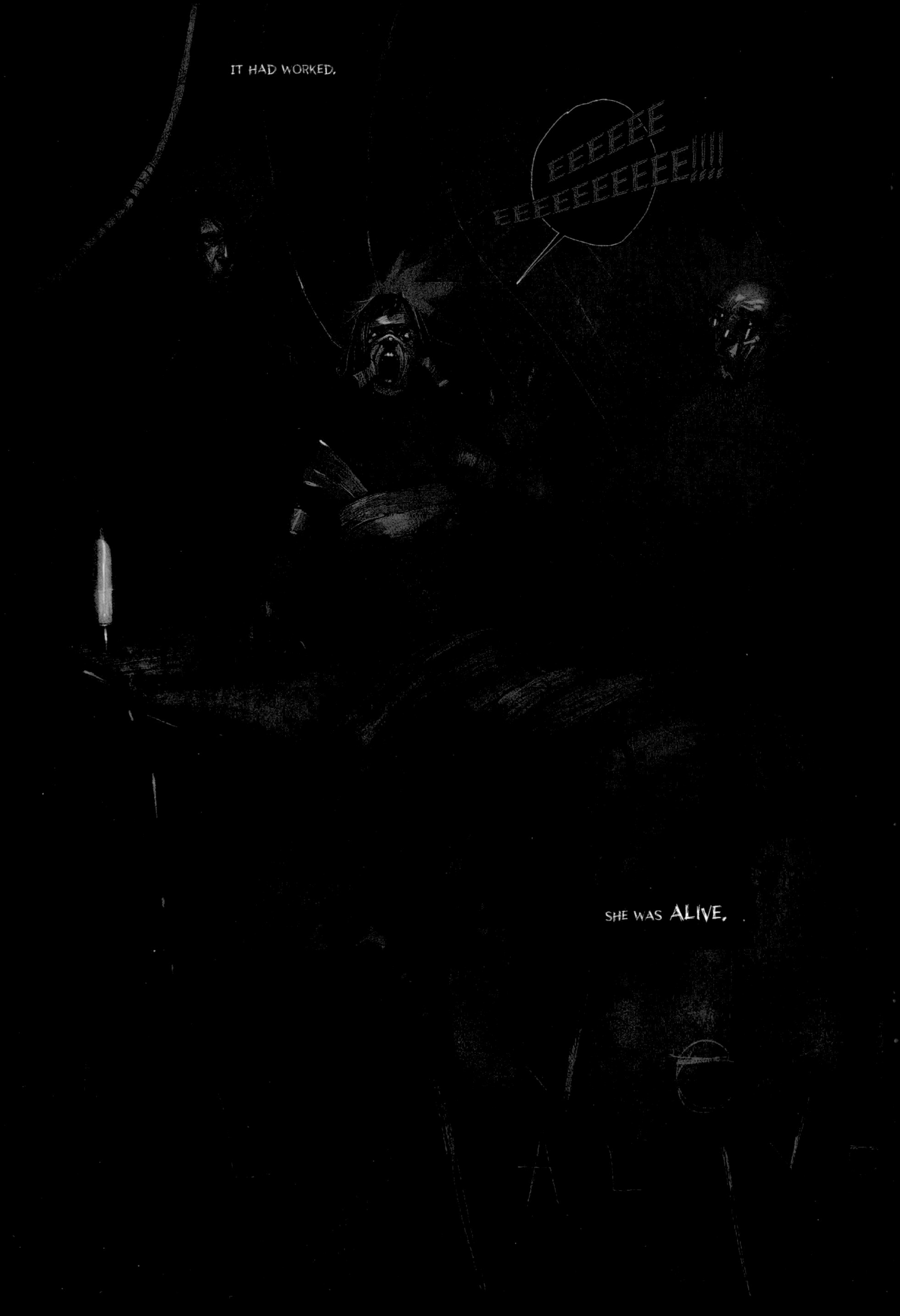
IT HAD WORKED.
EEEEEE EEEEEEEEEEE!!!!!
SHE WAS ALIVE.

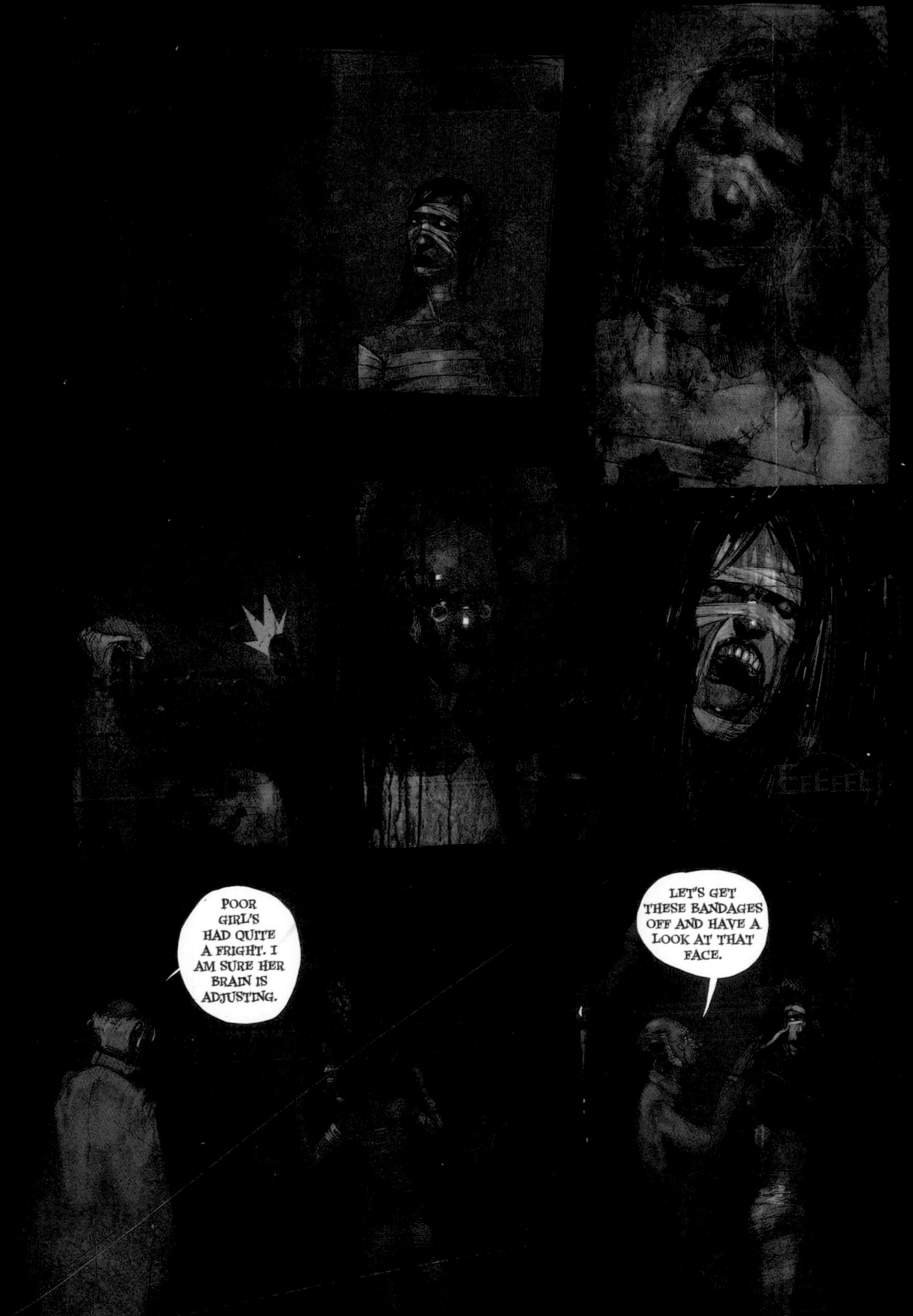
POOR GIRL'S HAD QUITE A FRIGHT. I AM SURE HER BRAIN IS ADJUSTING.
LET'S GET THESE BANDAGES OFF AND HAVE A LOOK AT THAT FACE.

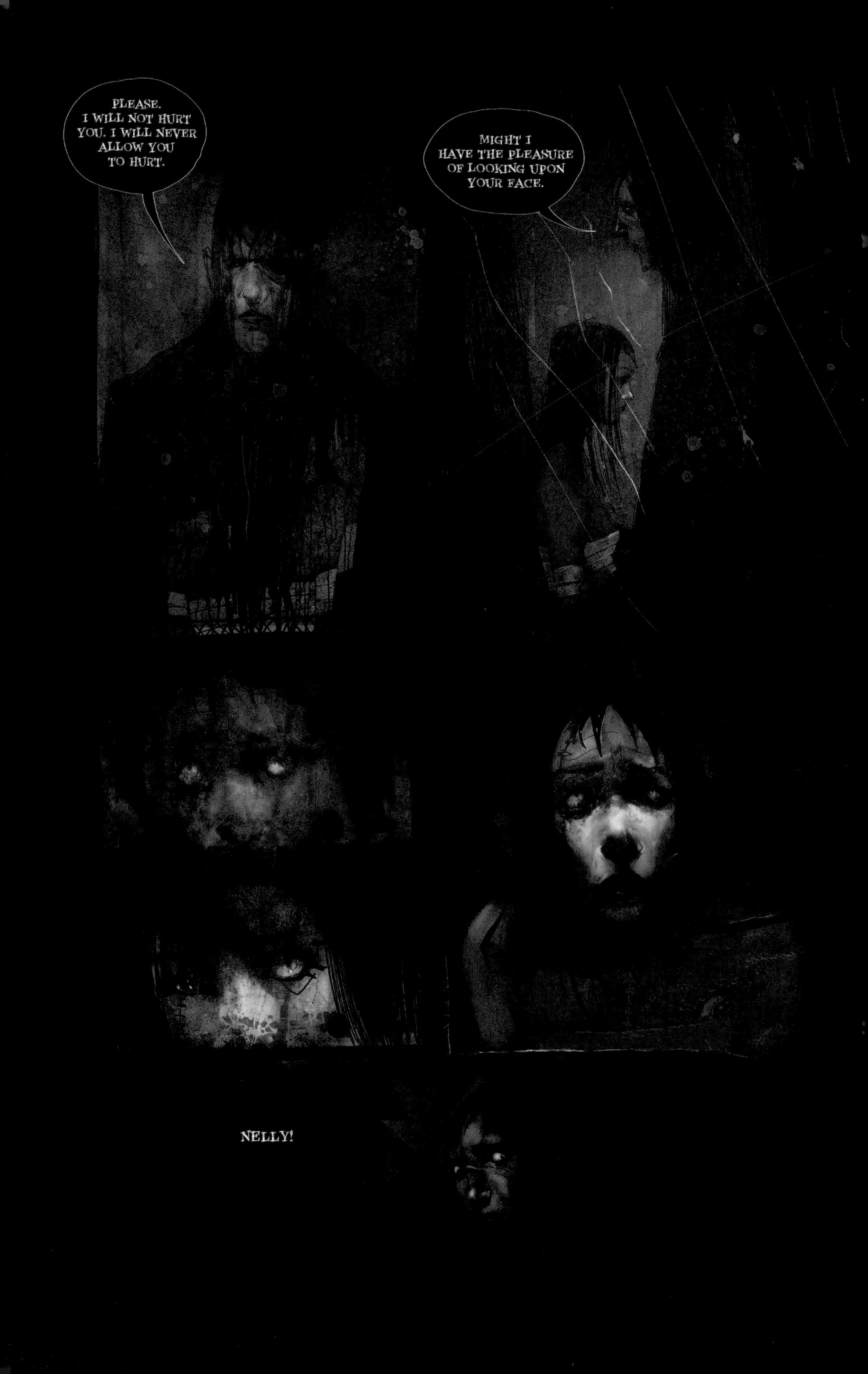
PLEASE. I WILL NOT HURT YOU. I WILL NEVER ALLOW YOU TO HURT.
MIGHT I HAVE THE PLEASURE OF LOOKING UPON YOUR FACE.
NELLY!

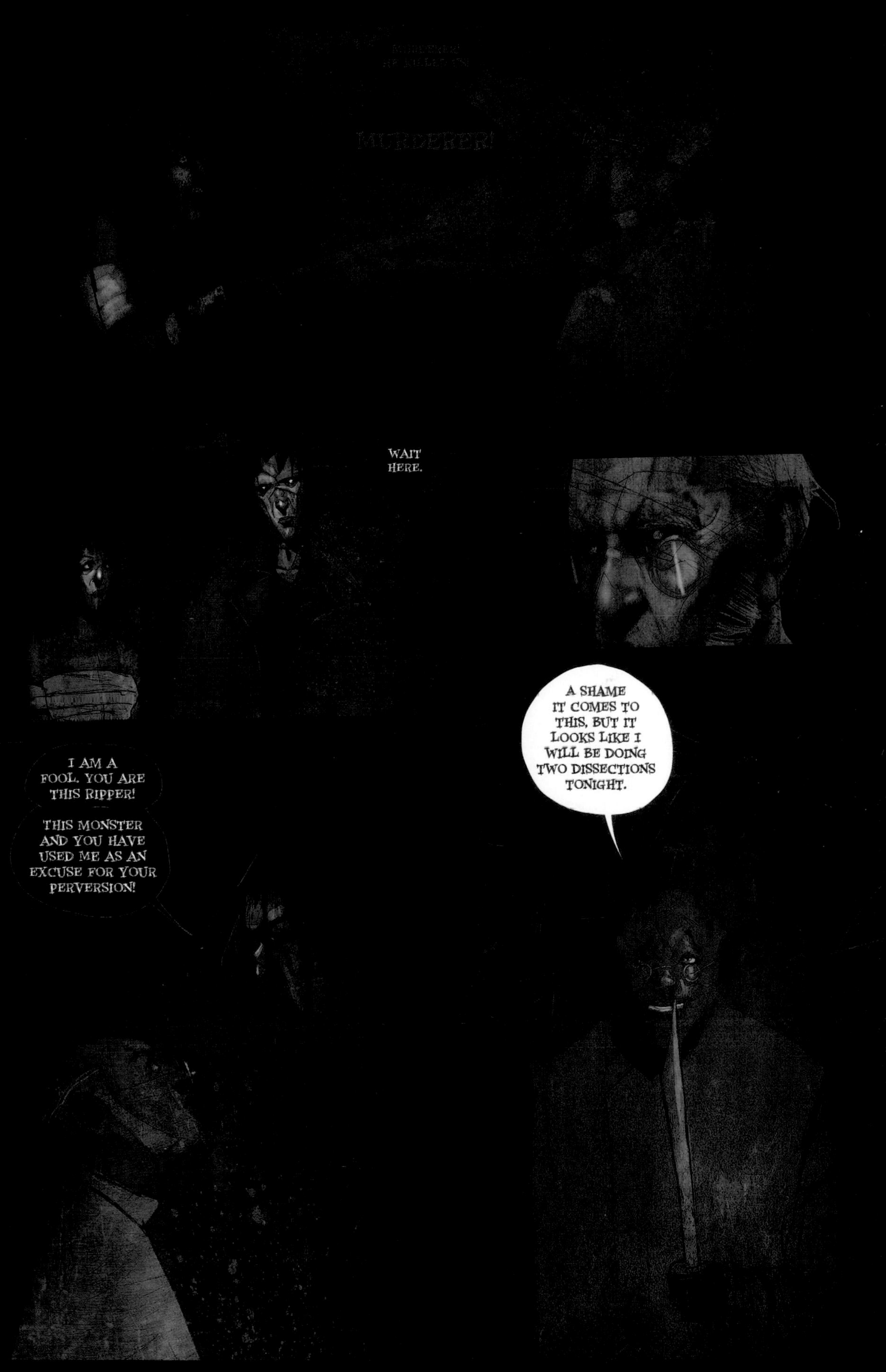
MURDERER!
WAIT HERE.
A SHAME IT COMES TO THIS, BUT IT LOOKS LIKE I WILL BE DOING TWO DISSECTIONS TONIGHT.
I AM A FOOL. YOU ARE THIS RIPPER!
THIS MONSTER AND YOU HAVE USED ME AS AN EXCUSE FOR YOUR PERVERSION!

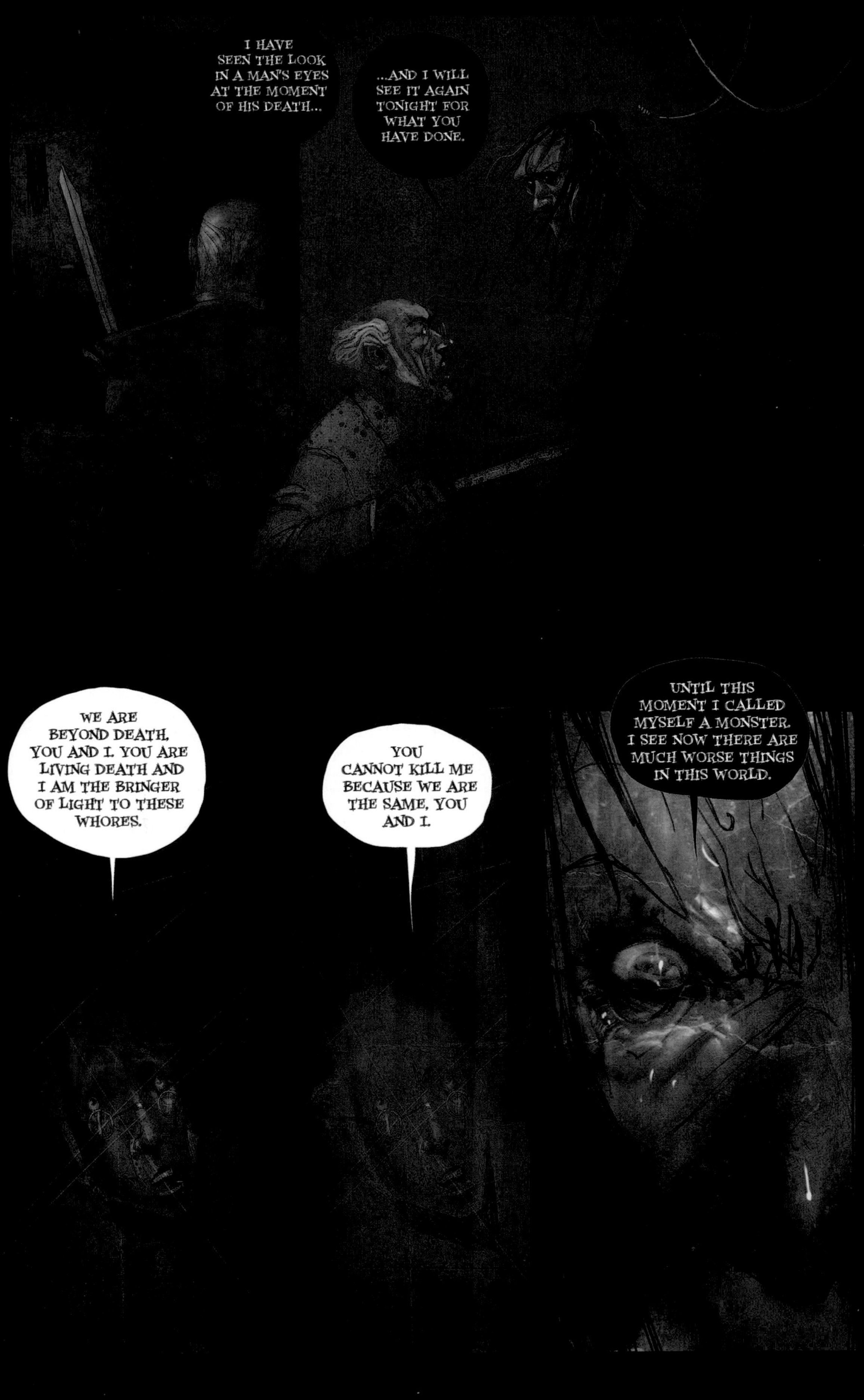
I HAVE SEEN THE LOOK IN A MAN'S EYES AT THE MOMENT OF HIS DEATH...
...AND I WILL SEE IT AGAIN TONIGHT FOR WHAT YOU HAVE DONE.
WE ARE BEYOND DEATH, YOU AND I. YOU ARE LIVING DEATH AND I AM THE BRINGER OF LIGHT TO THESE WHORES.
YOU CANNOT KILL ME BECAUSE WE ARE THE SAME, YOU AND I.
UNTIL THIS MOMENT I CALLED MYSELF A MONSTER. I SEE NOW THERE ARE MUCH WORSE THINGS IN THIS WORLD.

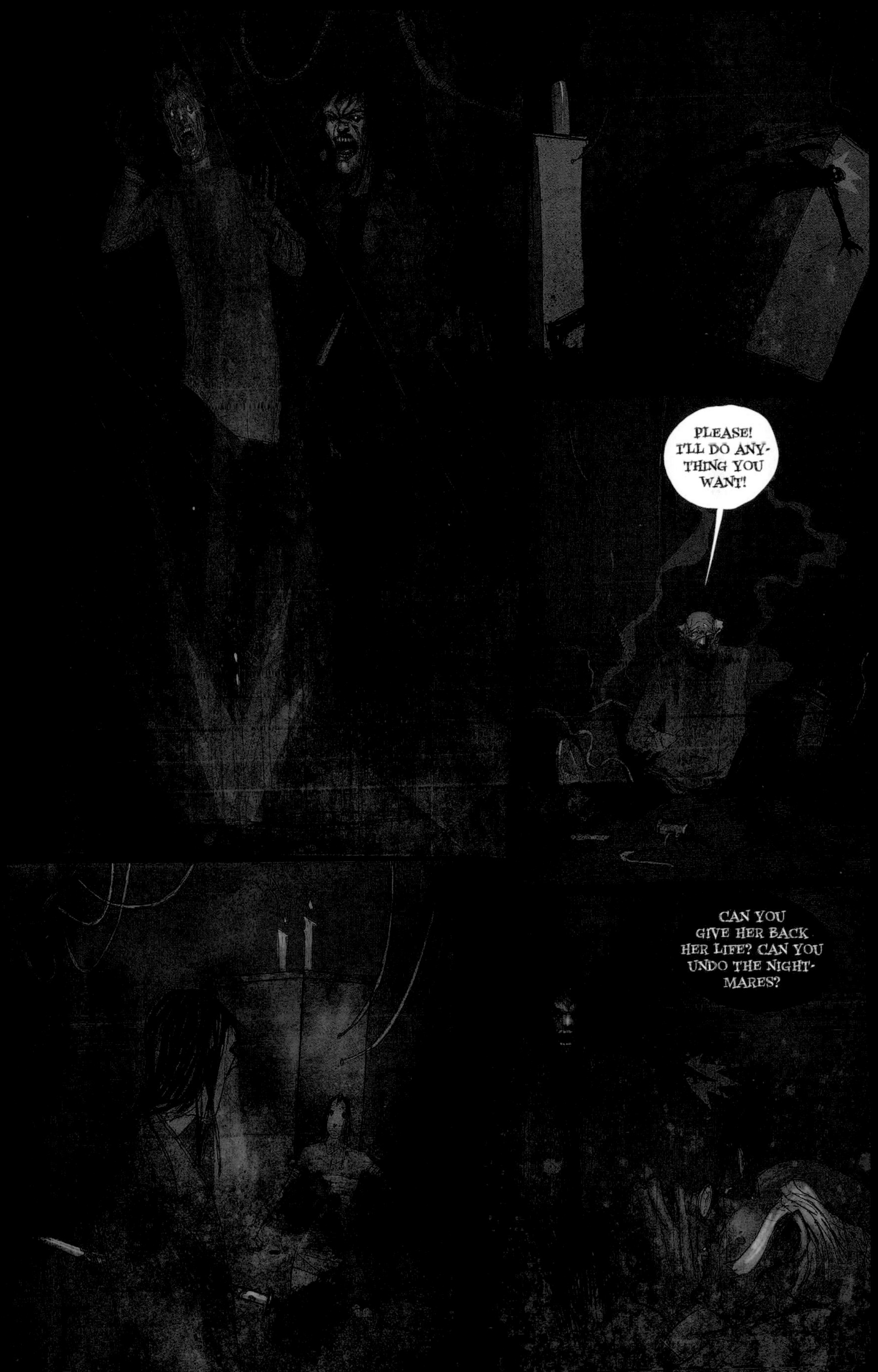
PLEASE! I'LL DO ANYTHING YOU WANT!
CAN YOU GIVE HER BACK HER LIFE? CAN YOU UNDO THE NIGHTMARES?

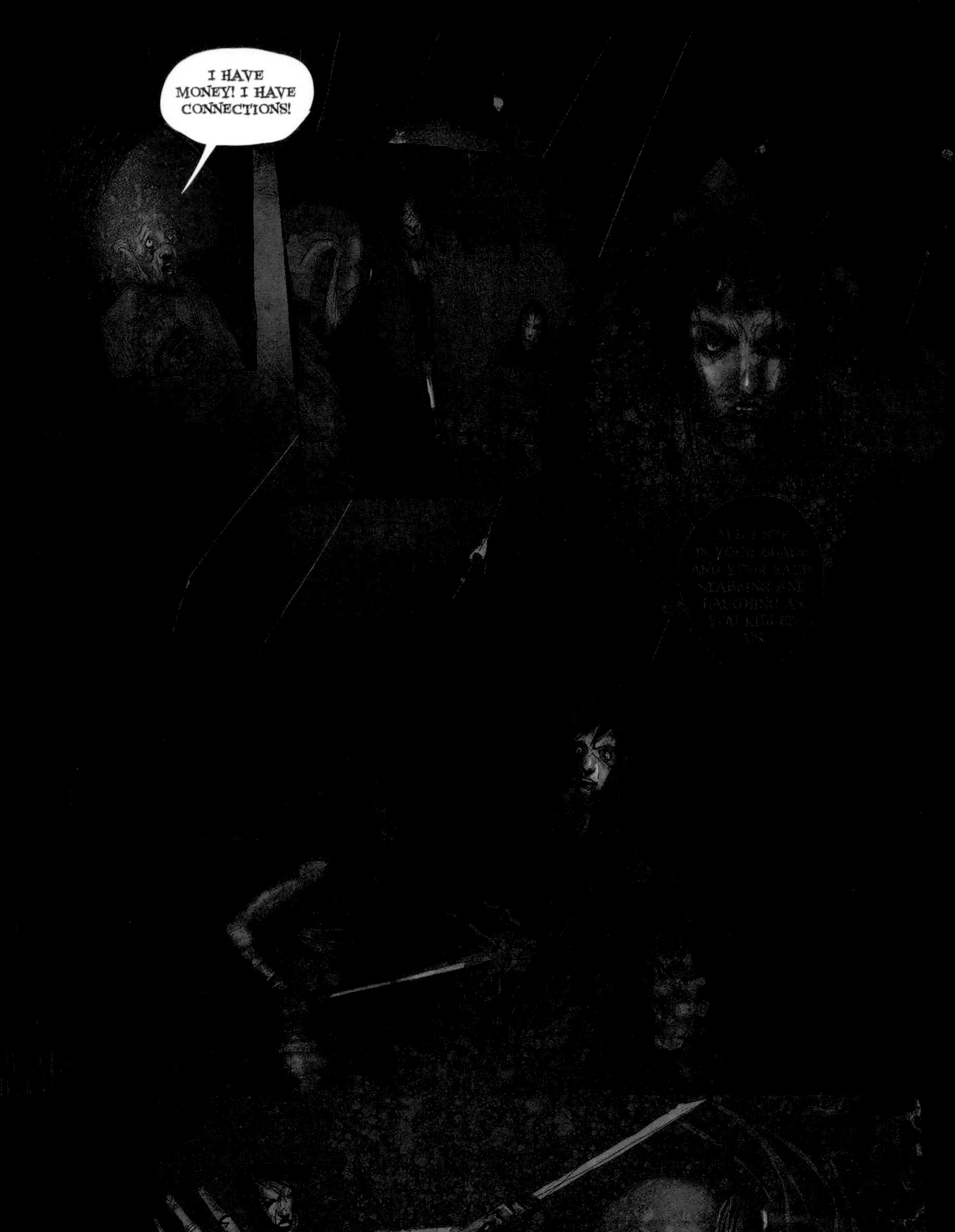
I HAVE MONEY! I HAVE CONNECTIONS!

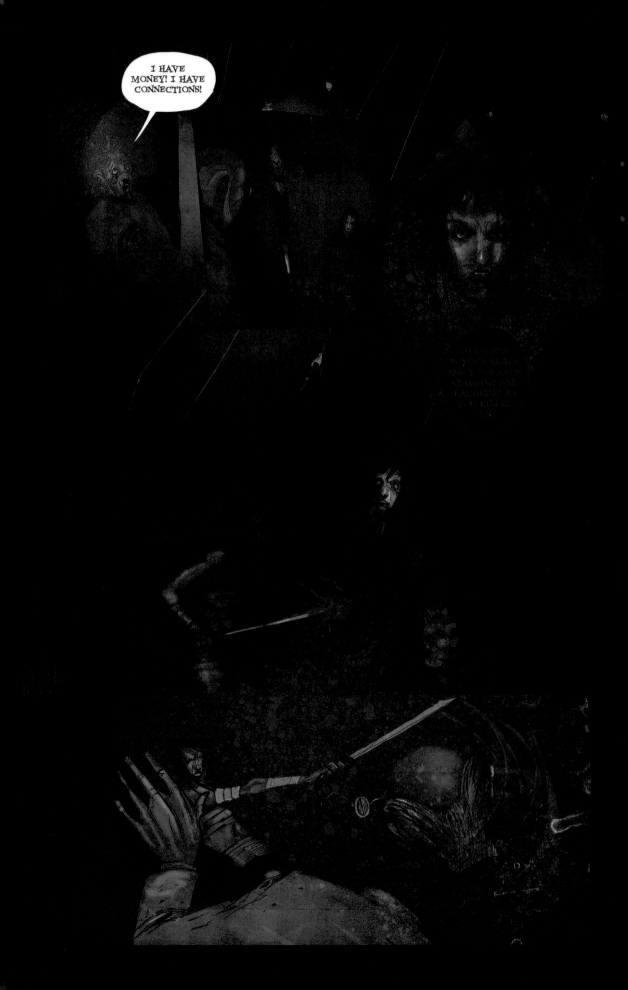

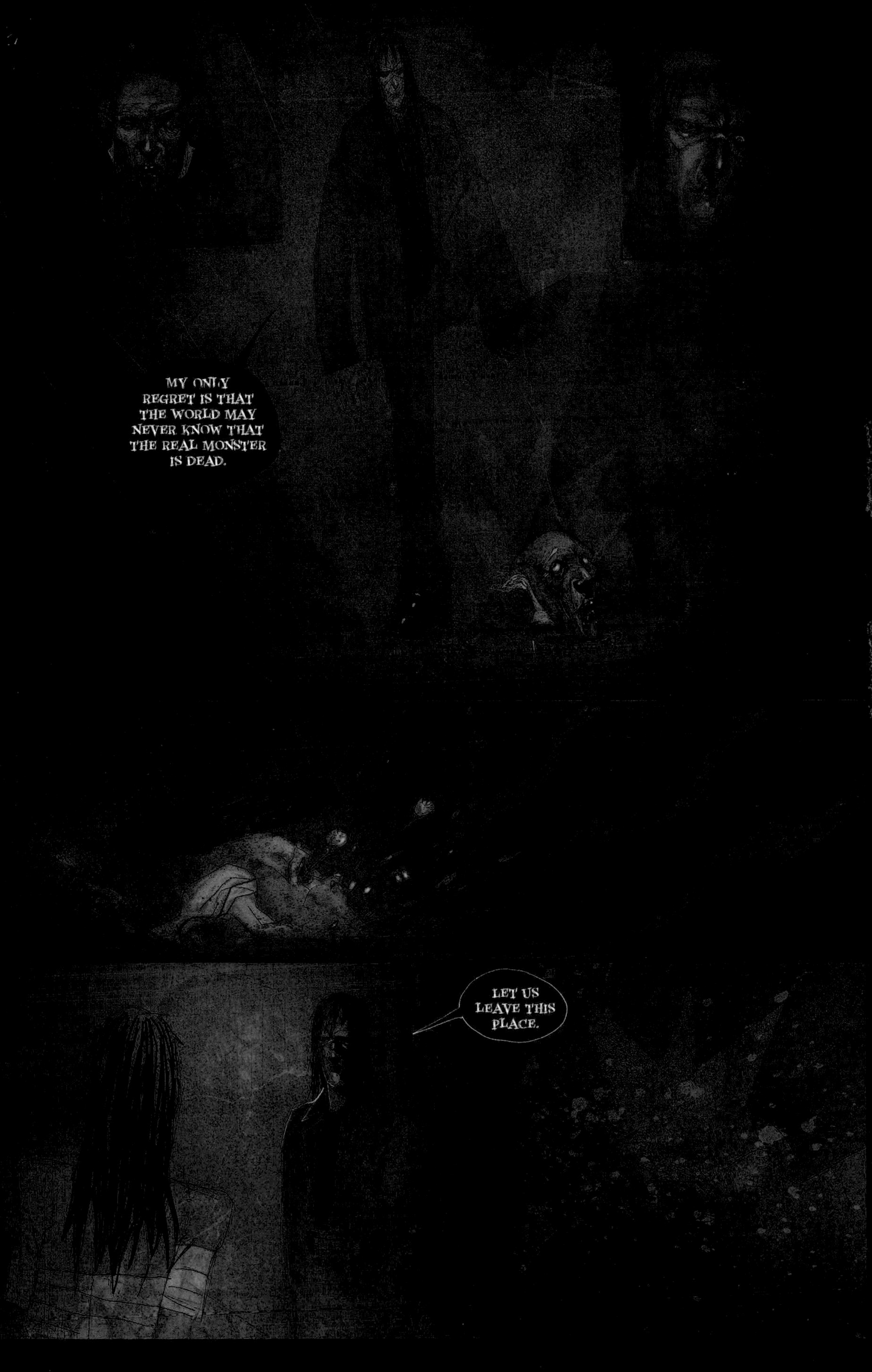
MY ONLY REGRET IS THAT THE WORLD MAY NEVER KNOW THAT THE REAL MONSTER IS DEAD.
LET US LEAVE THIS PLACE.

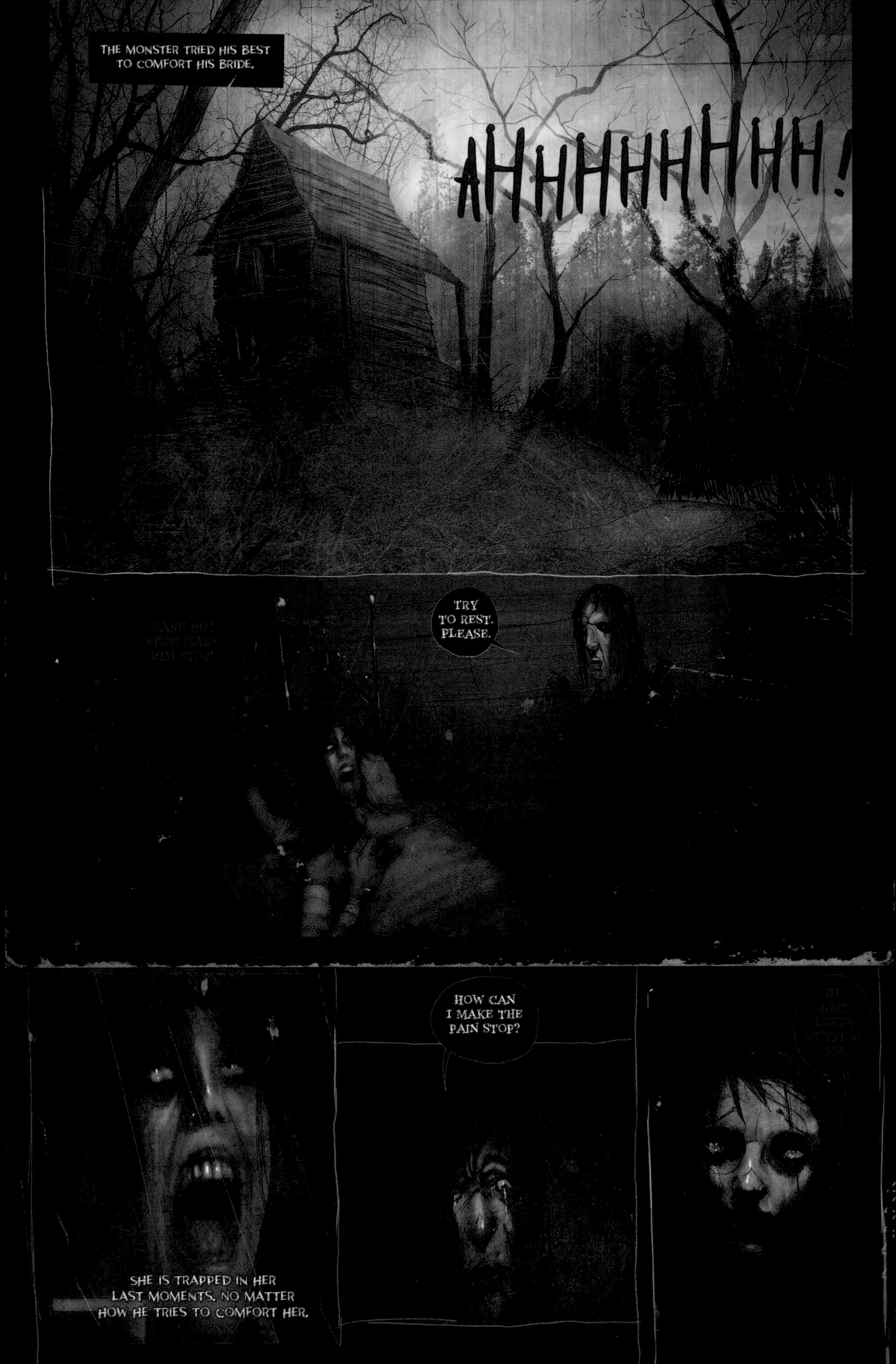
THE MONSTER TRIED HIS BEST TO COMFORT HIS BRIDE.
AHHHHHHHH!
MAKE HIM STOP MAKE HIM STOP
TRY TO REST. PLEASE.
HOW CAN I MAKE THE PAIN STOP?
SHE IS TRAPPED IN HER LAST MOMENTS, NO MATTER HOW HE TRIES TO COMFORT HER.

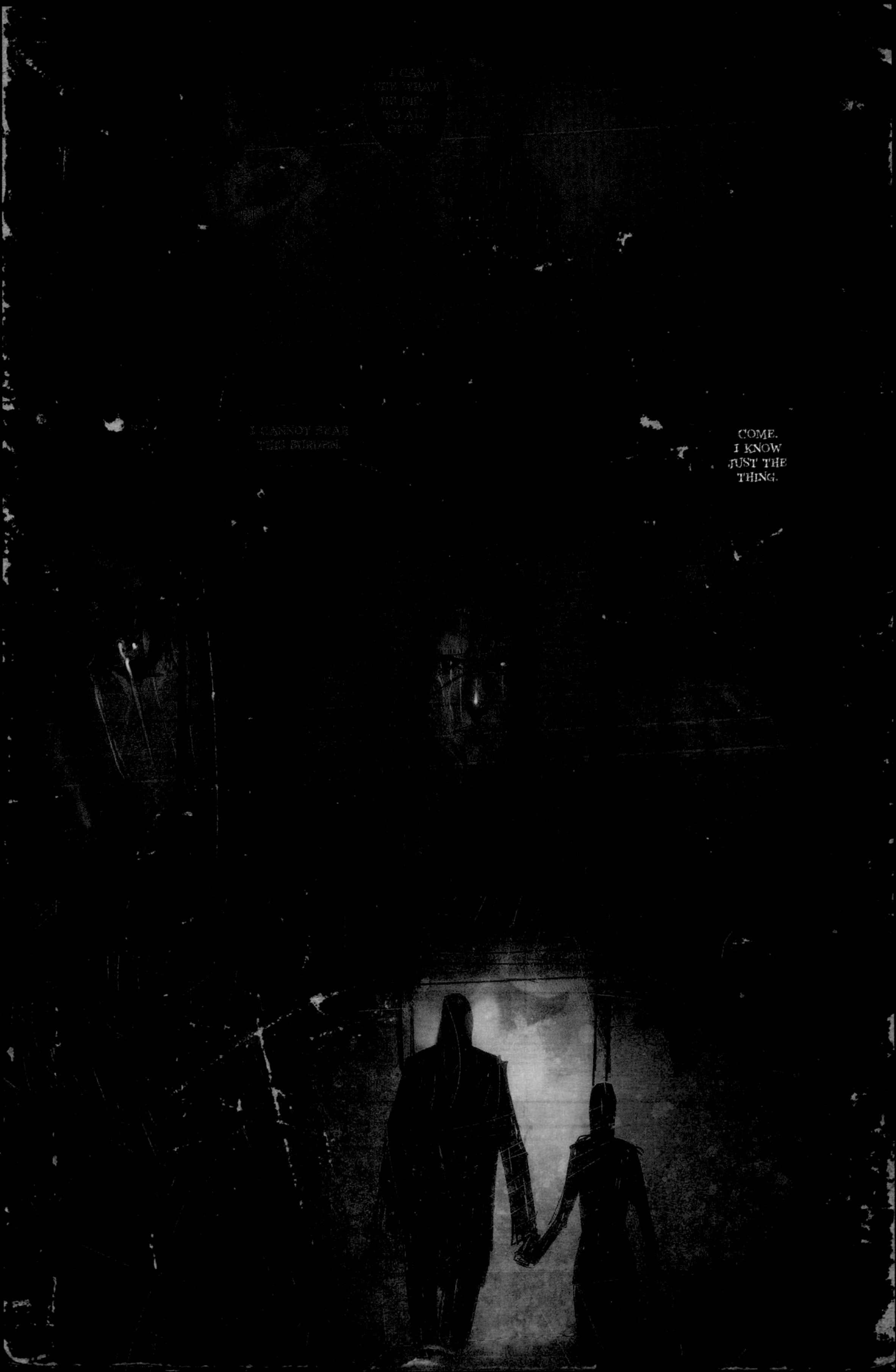
I CANNOT BEAR THIS BURDEN.
COME. I KNOW JUST THE THING.

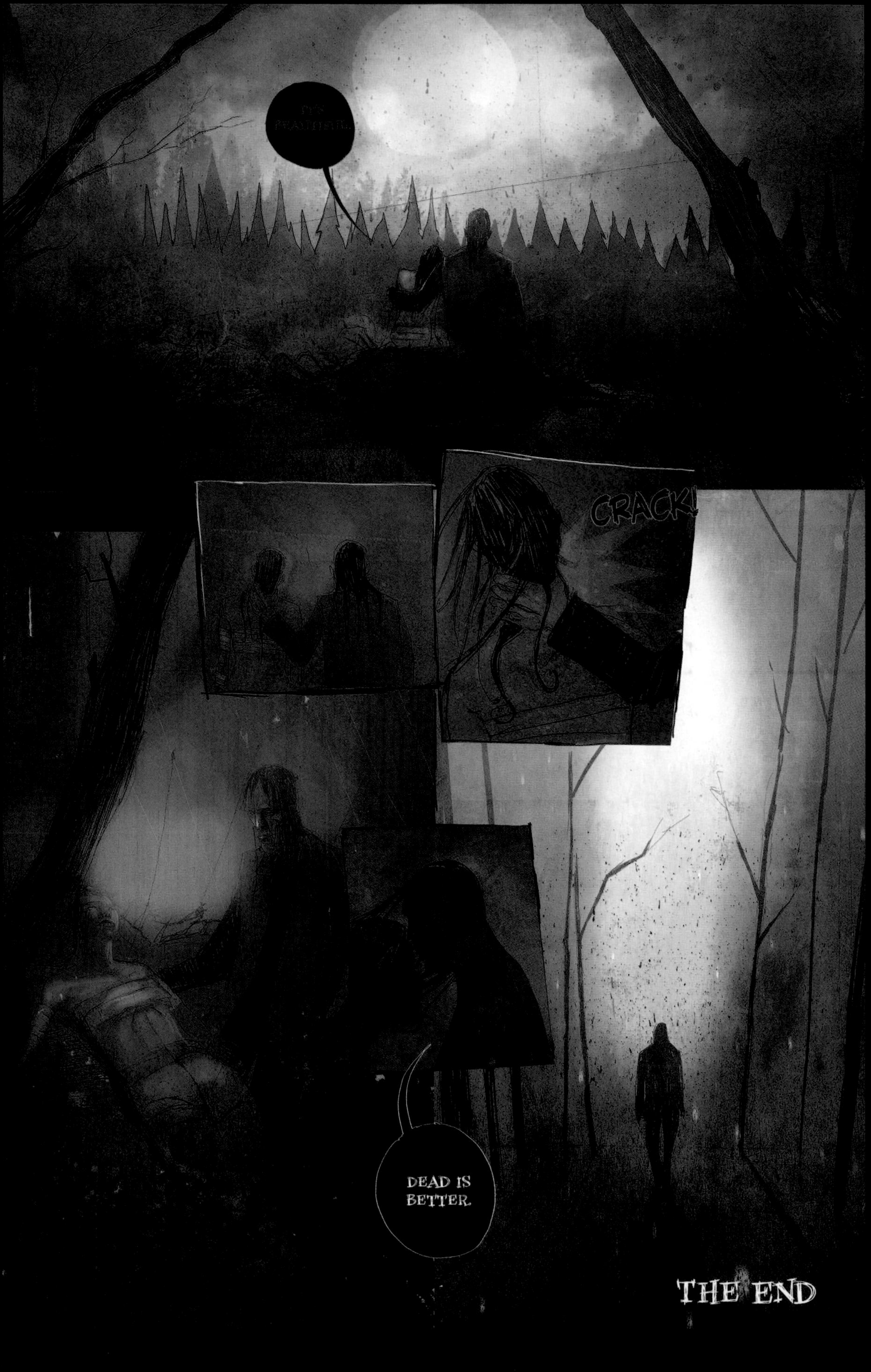
CRACK!
DEAD IS BETTER.
THE END

Art Gallery

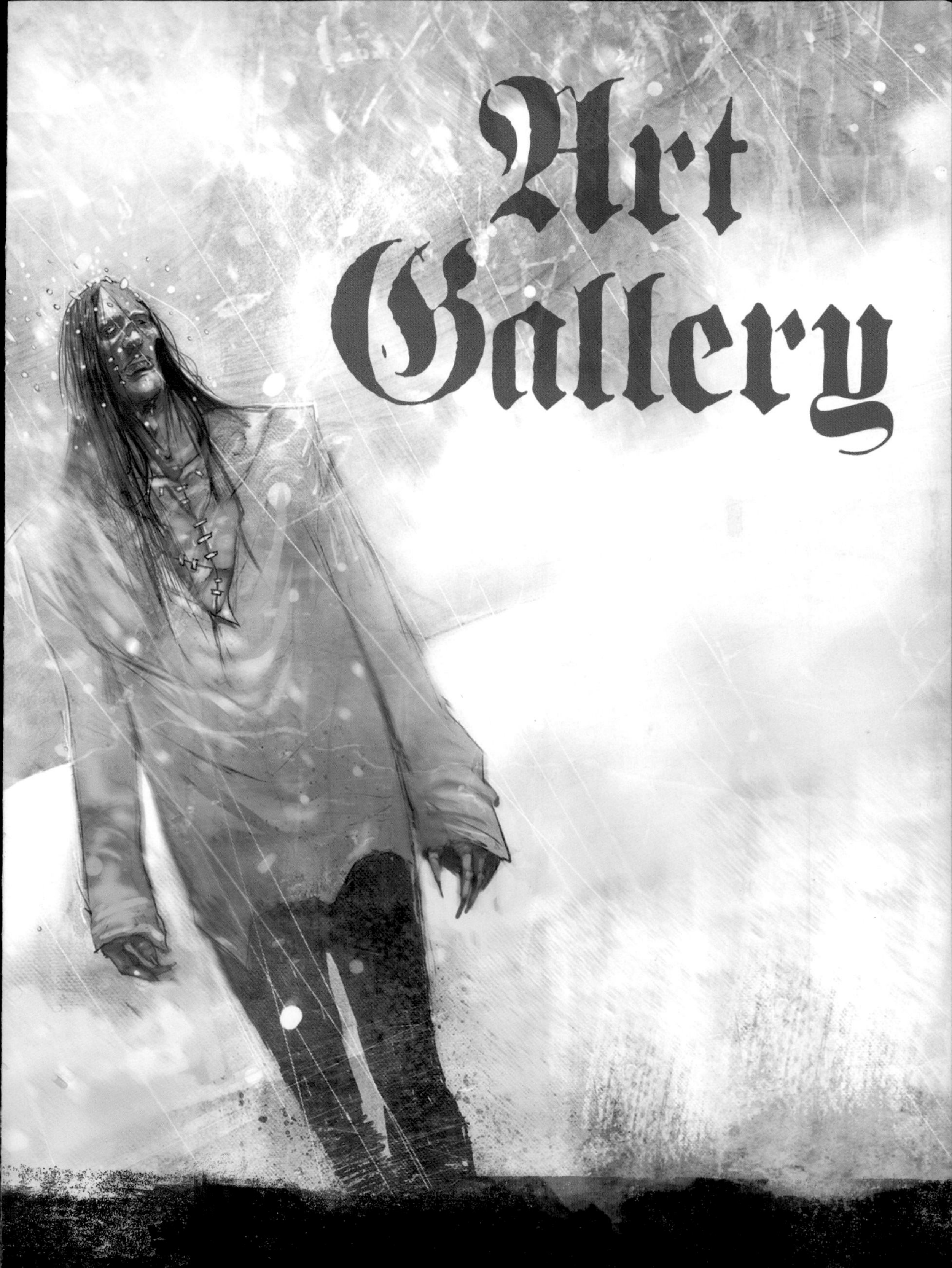

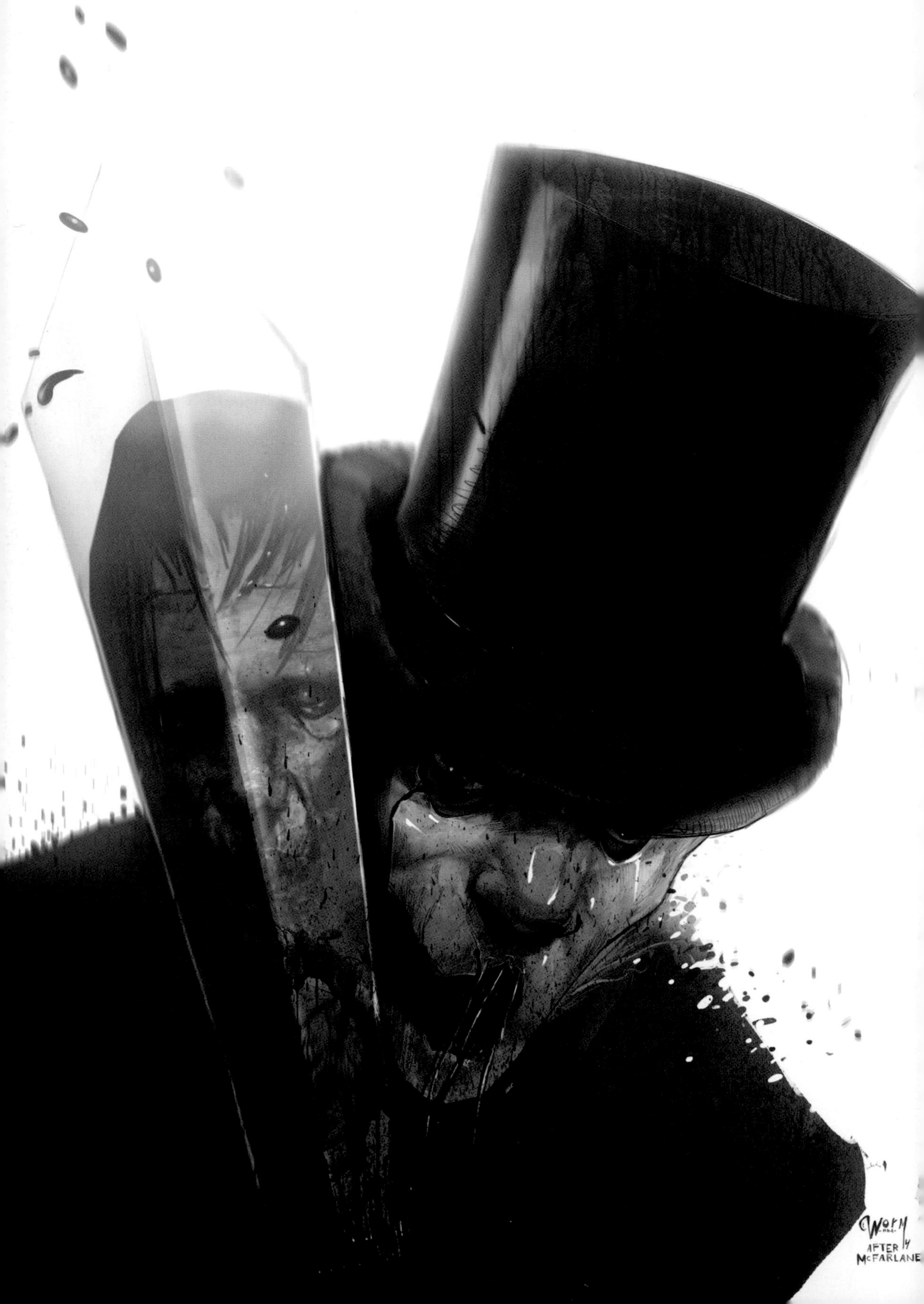
AFTER
McFARLANE

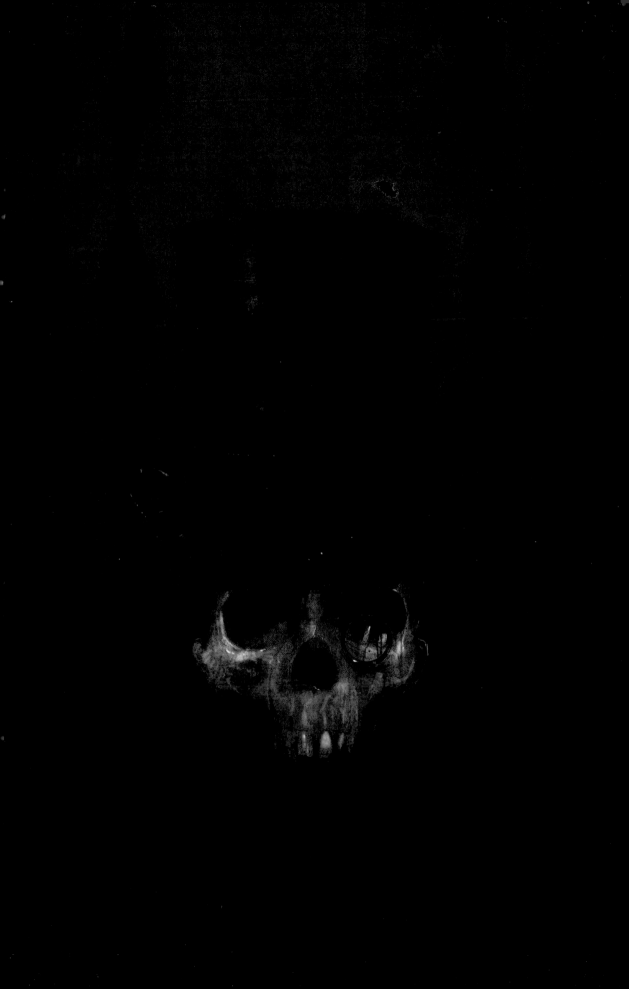

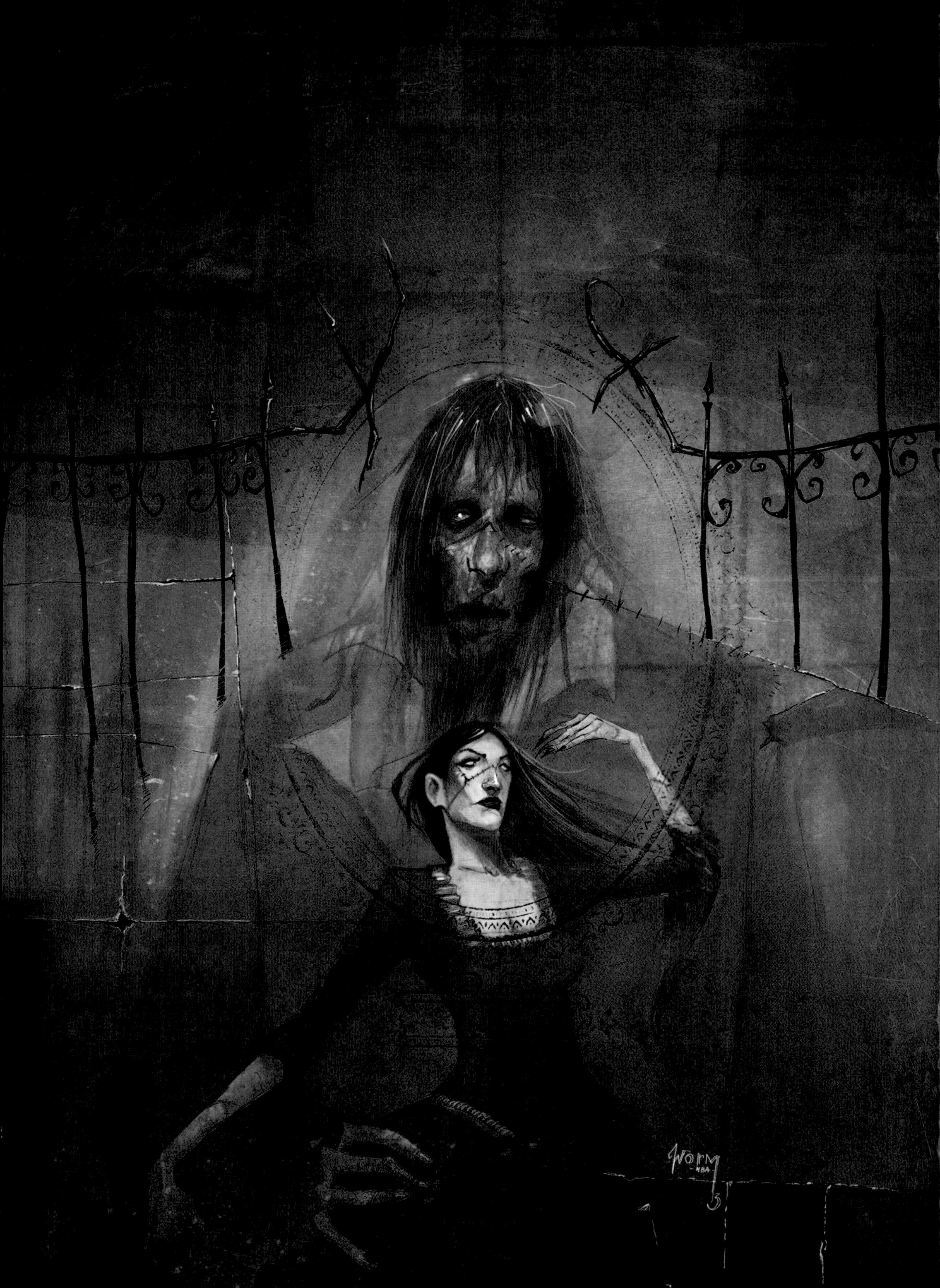

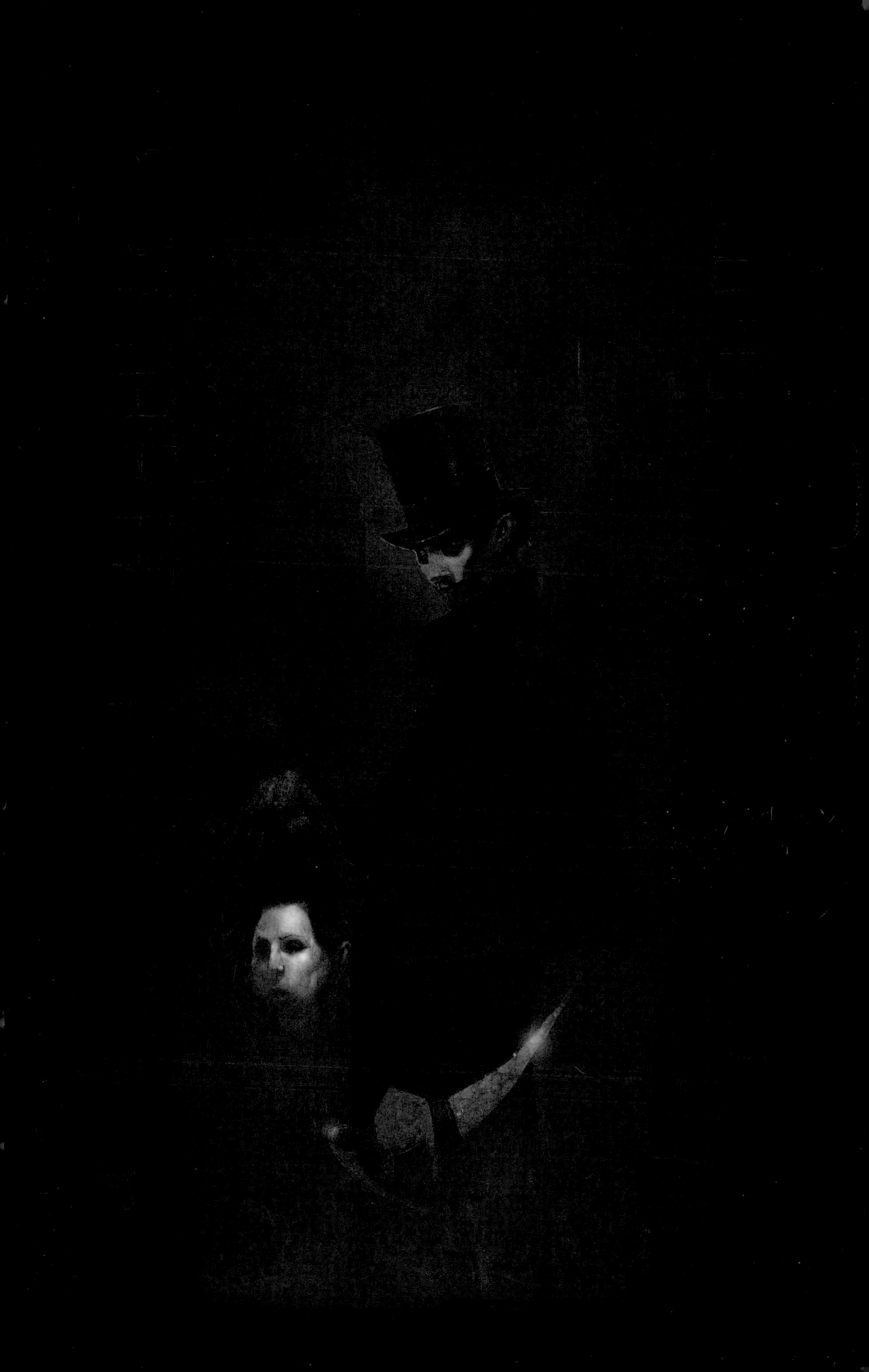

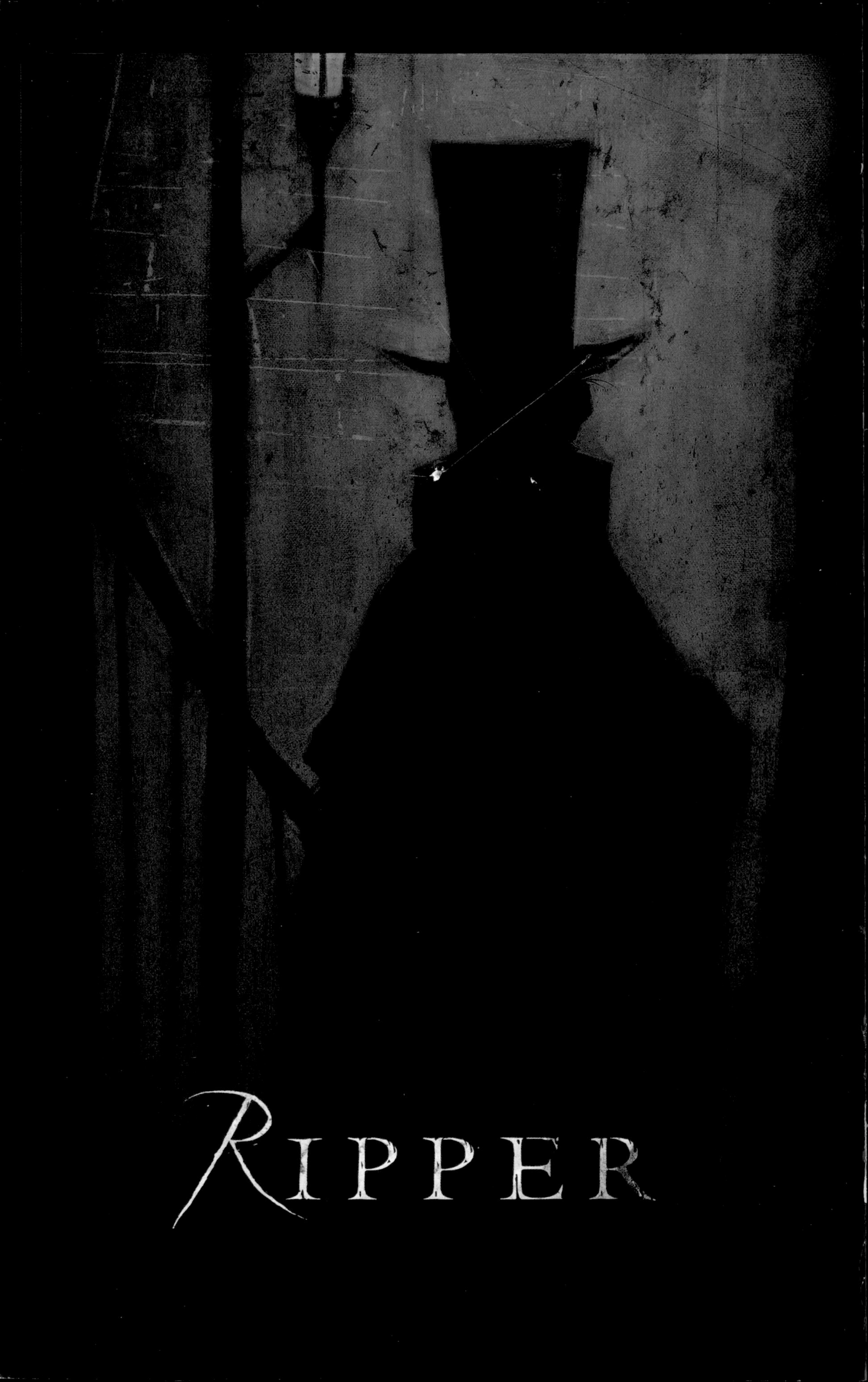

RIPPER

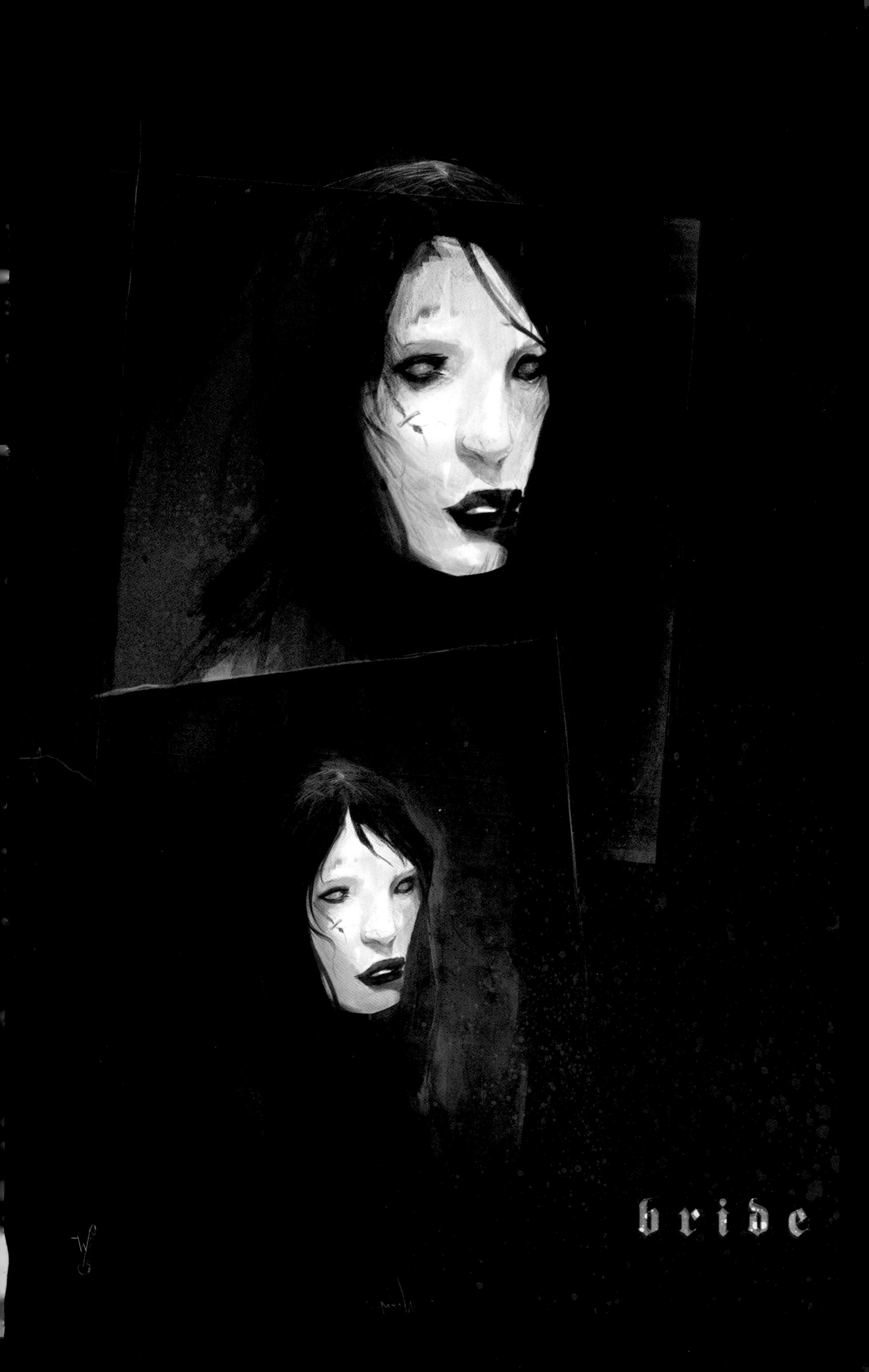
bride

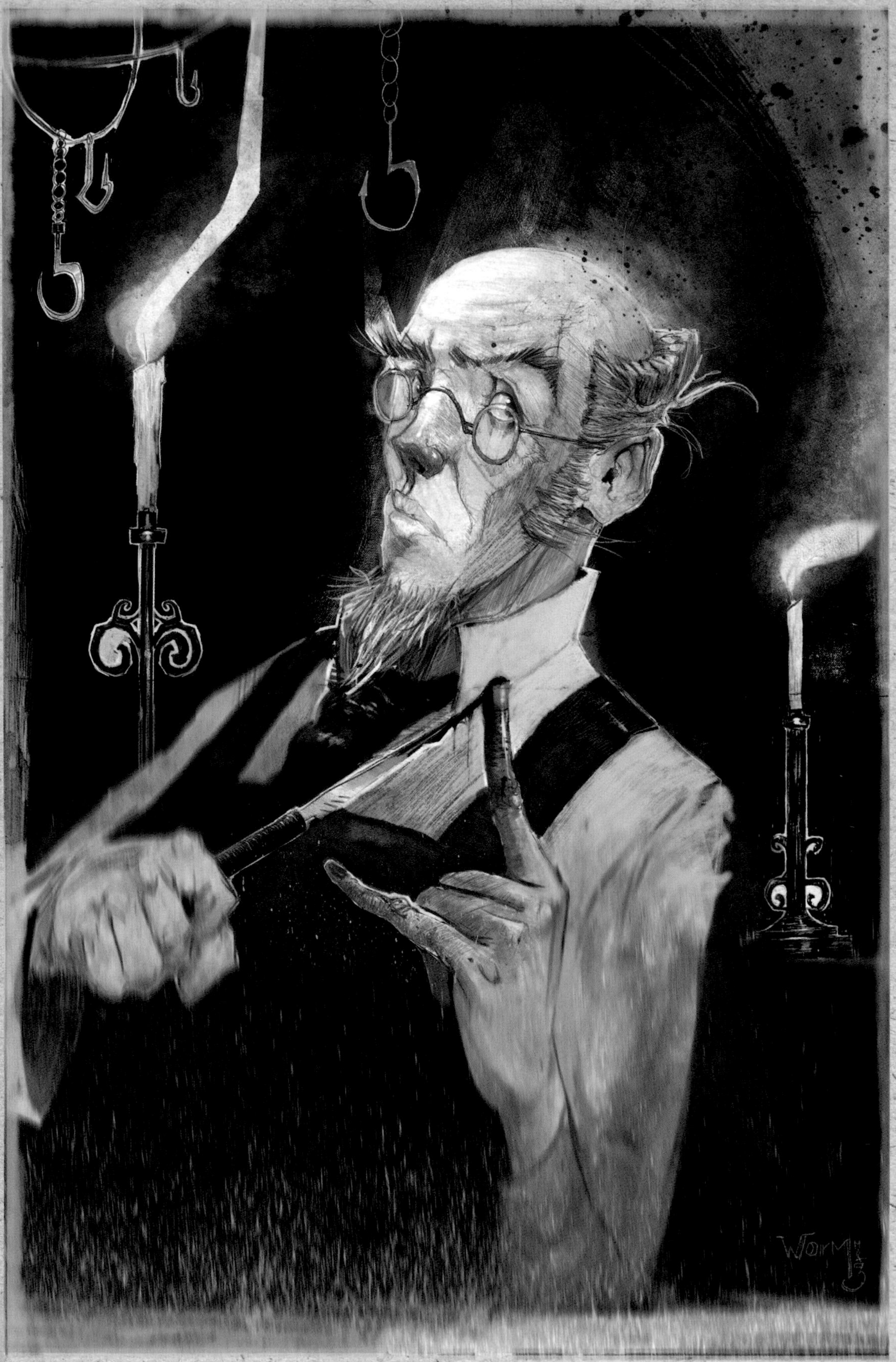

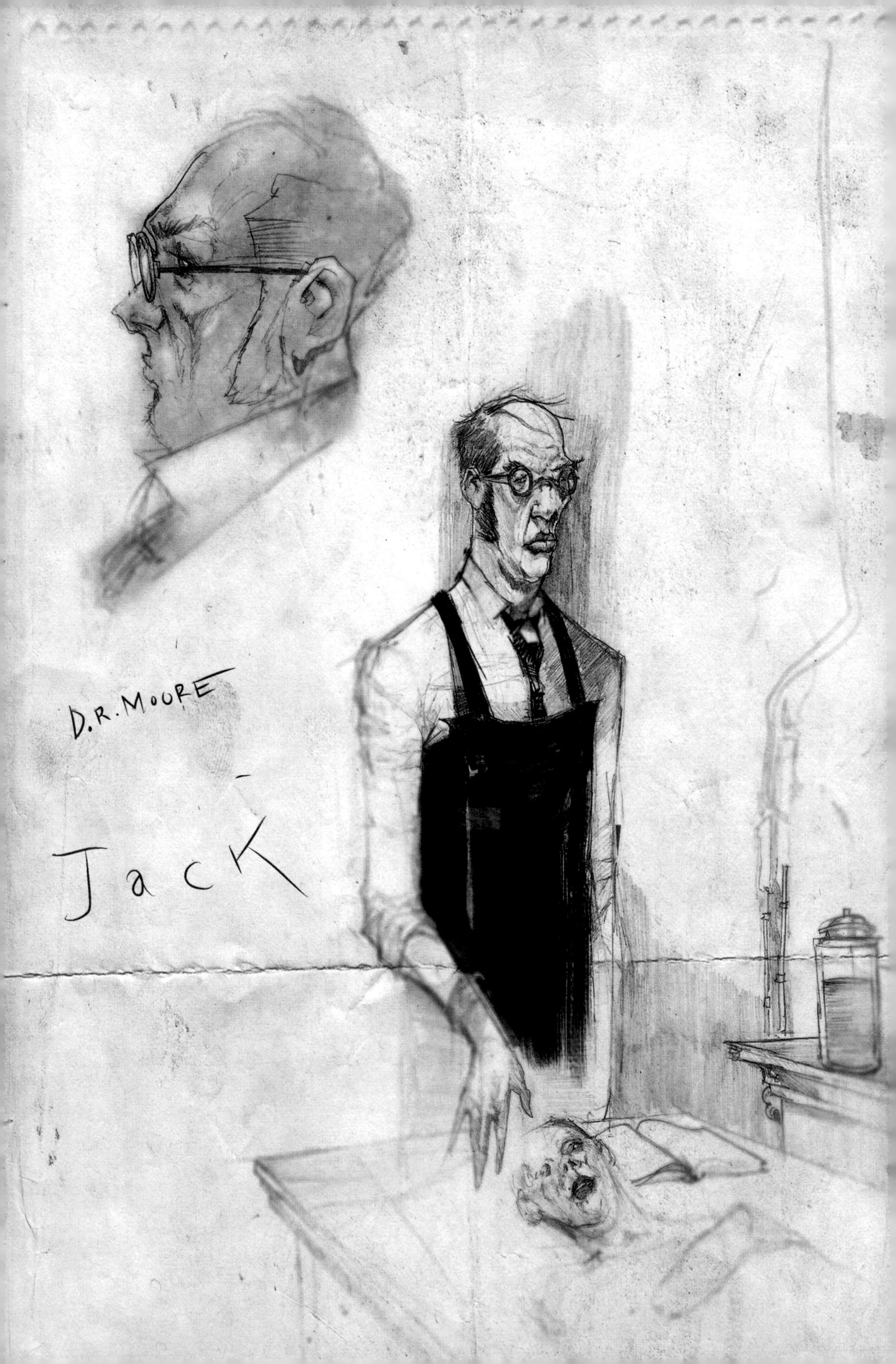
D.R. MOORE
Jack

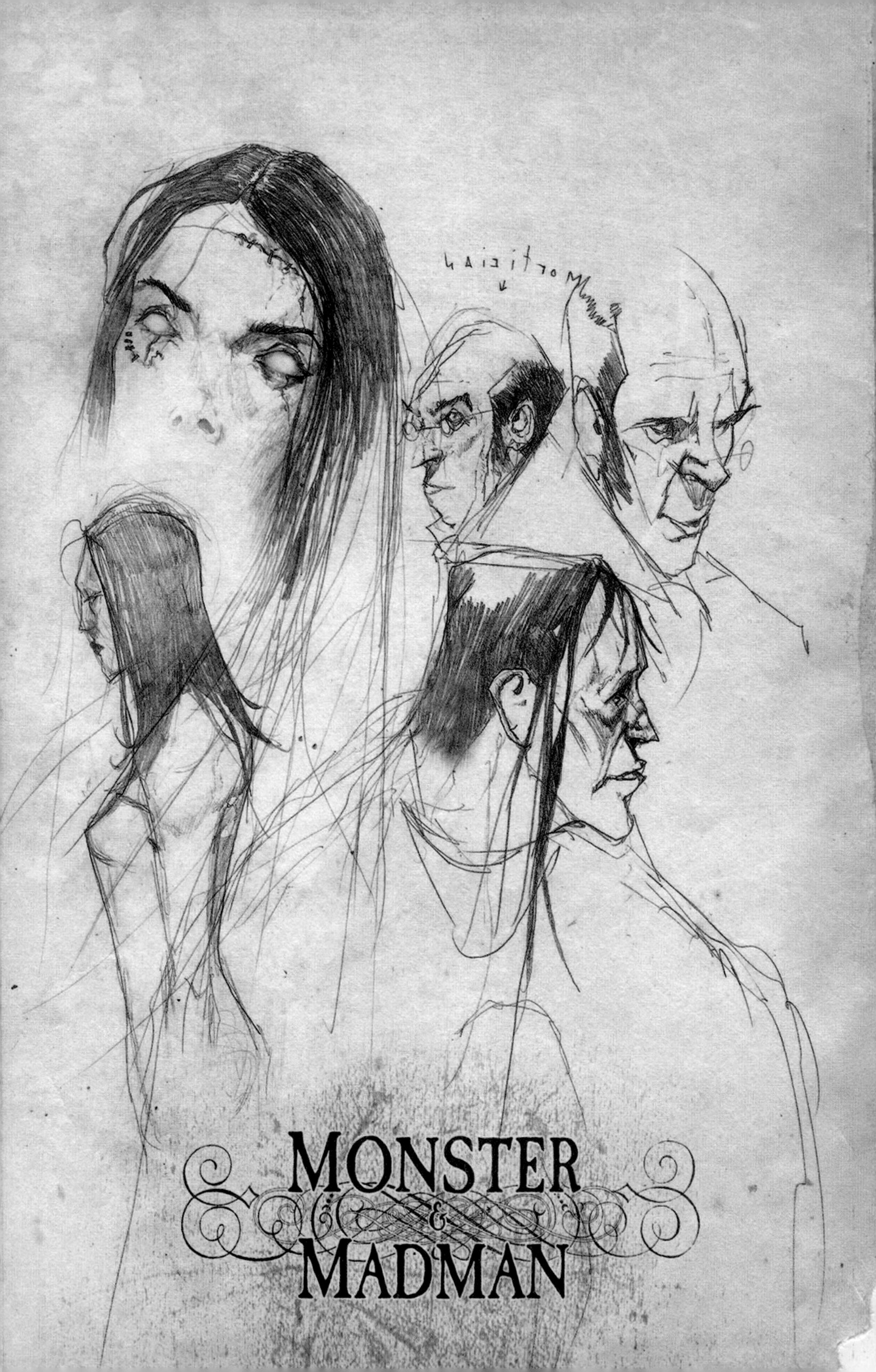
MONSTER
&
MADMAN

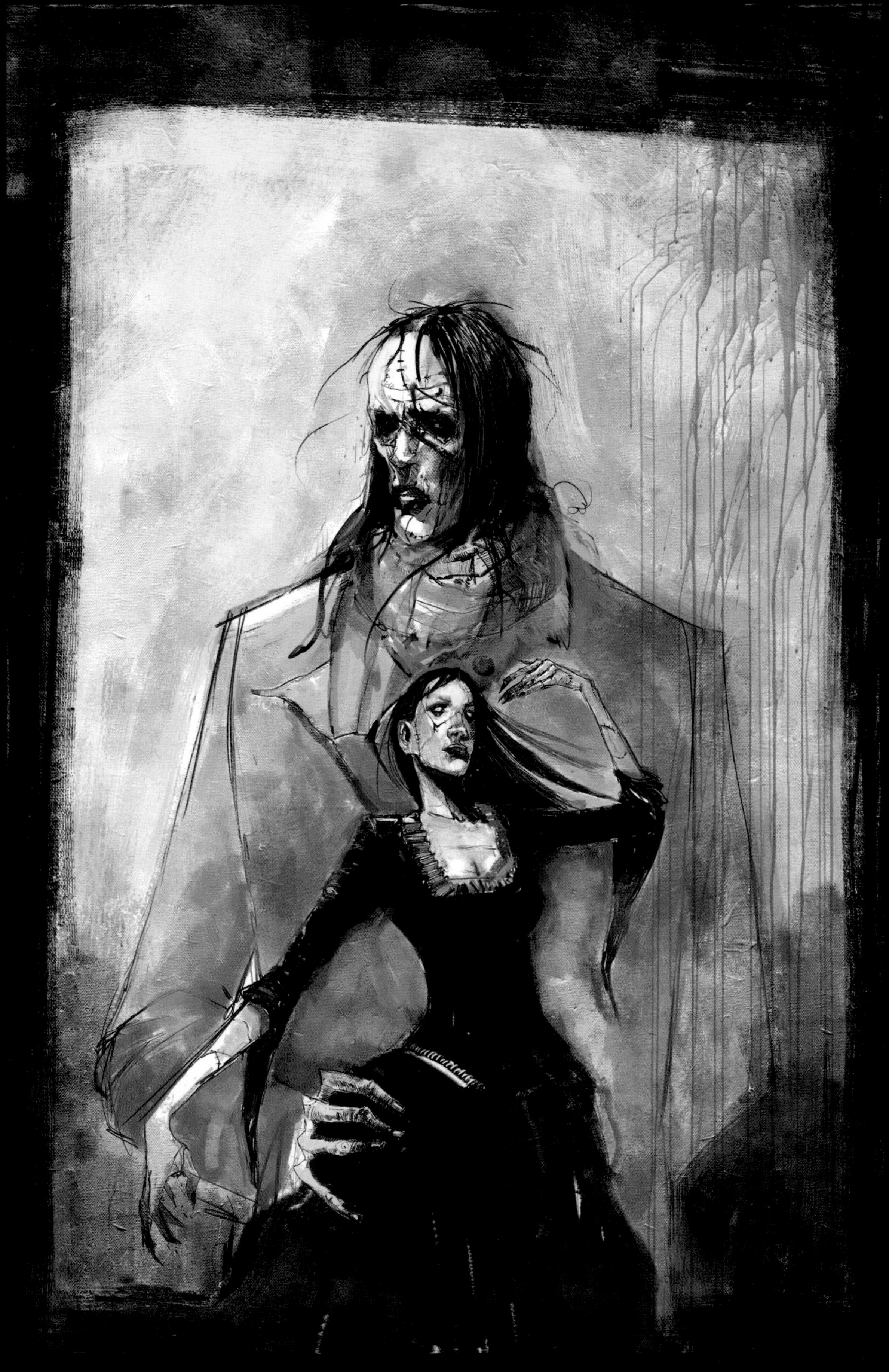

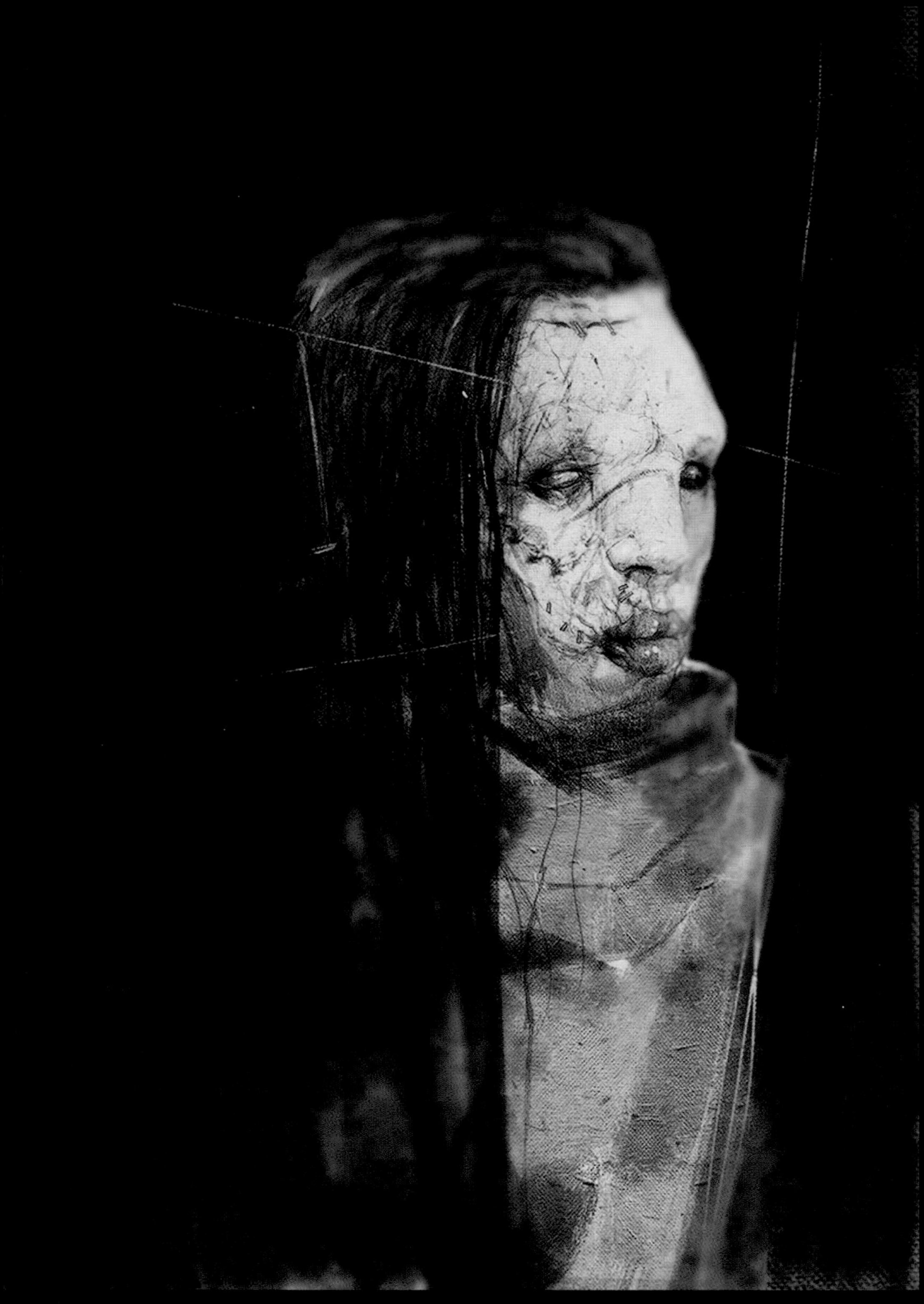

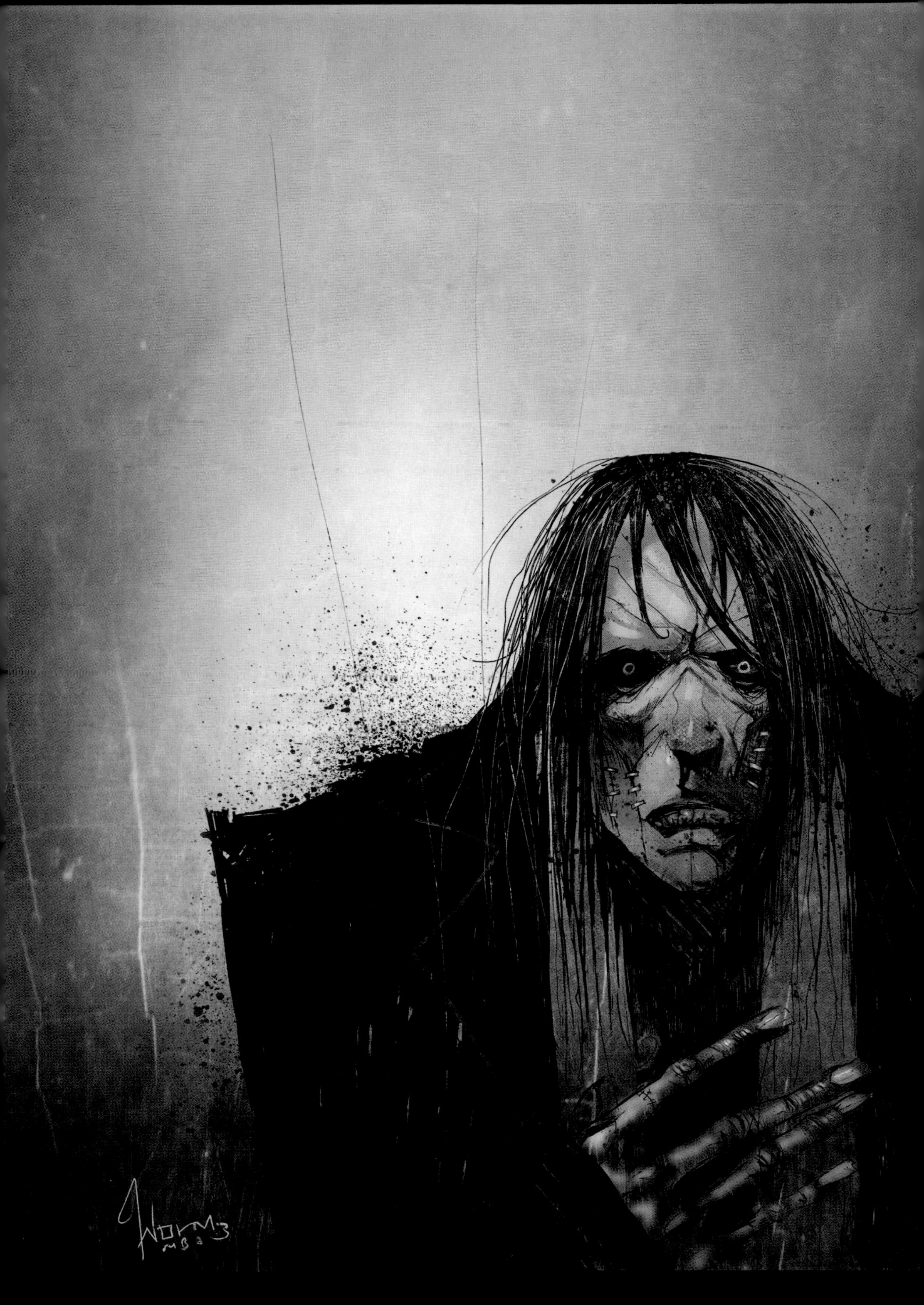

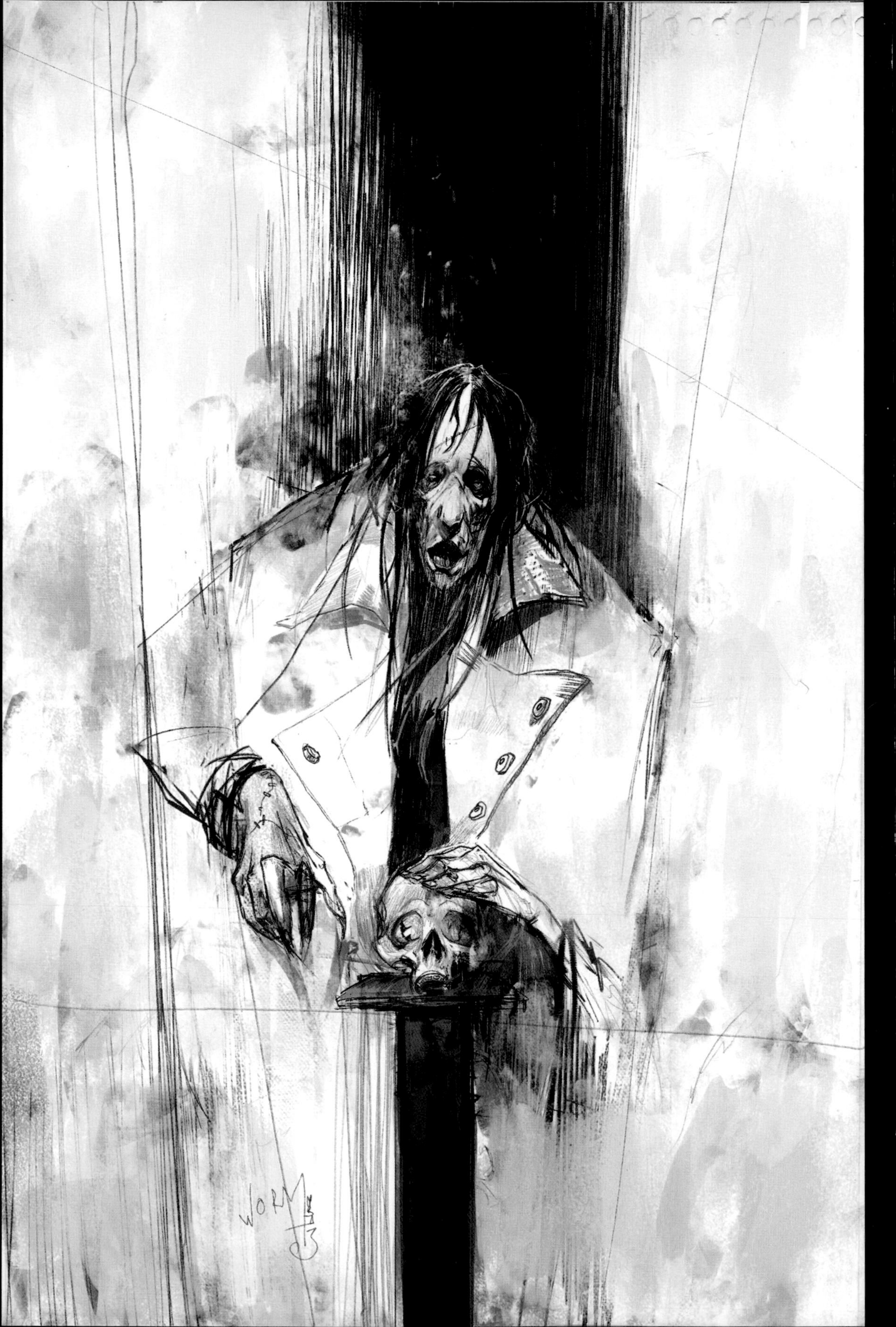
WORM

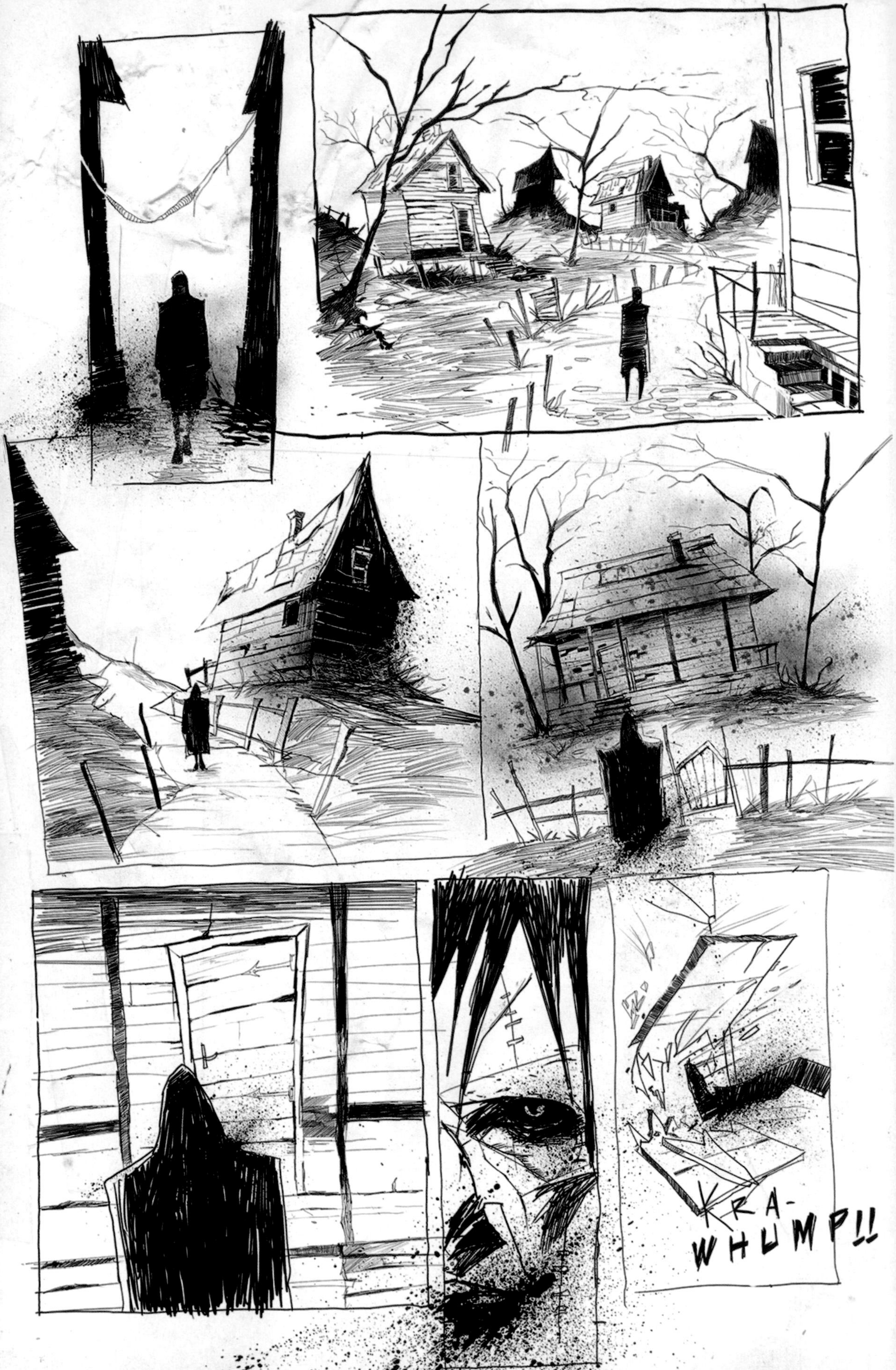
KRA-
WHUMP!!

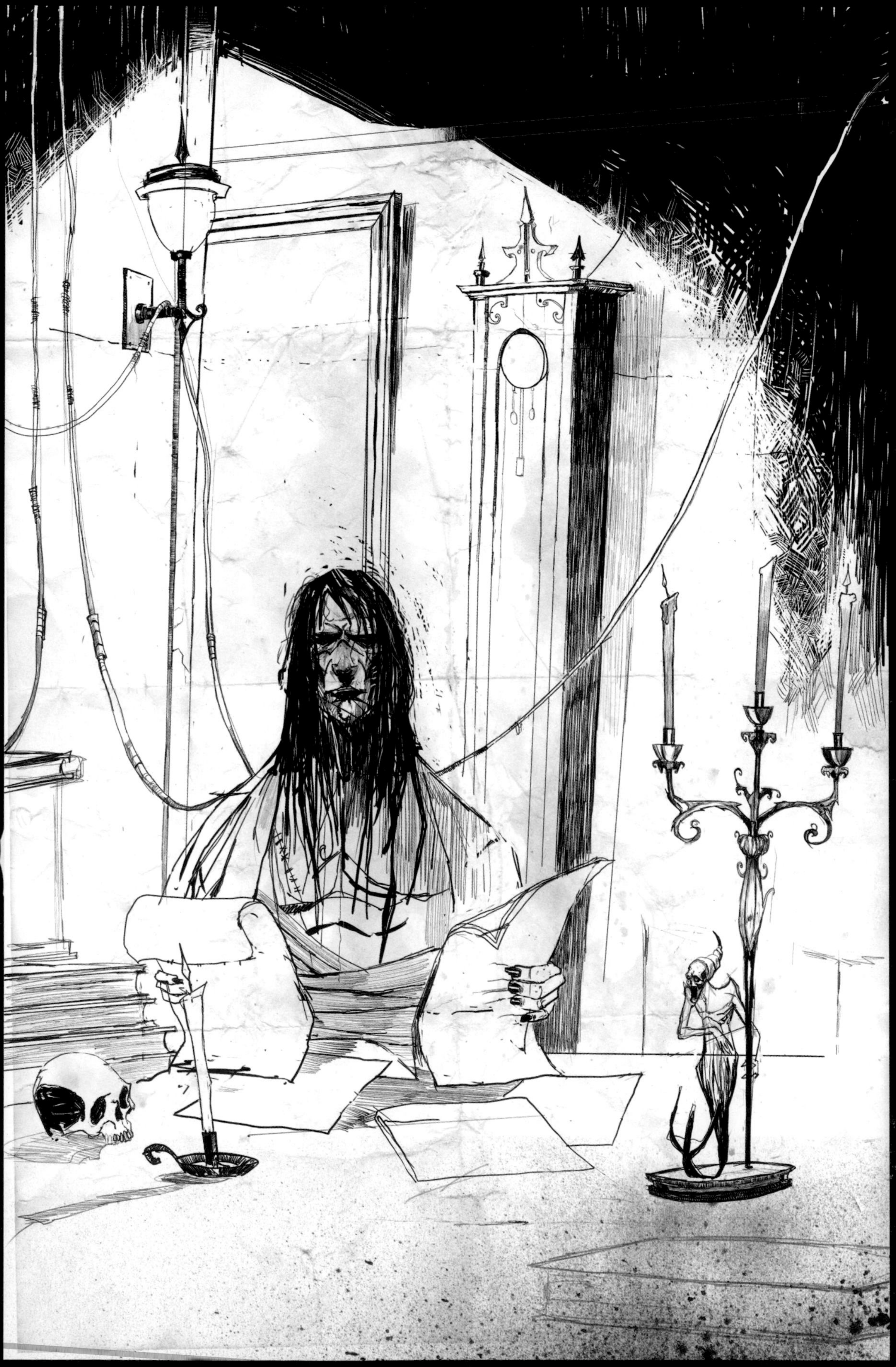

MONSTER & MADMAN

THE SECRET HISTORY *of* JACK THE RIPPER AND FRANKENSTEIN'S MONSTER

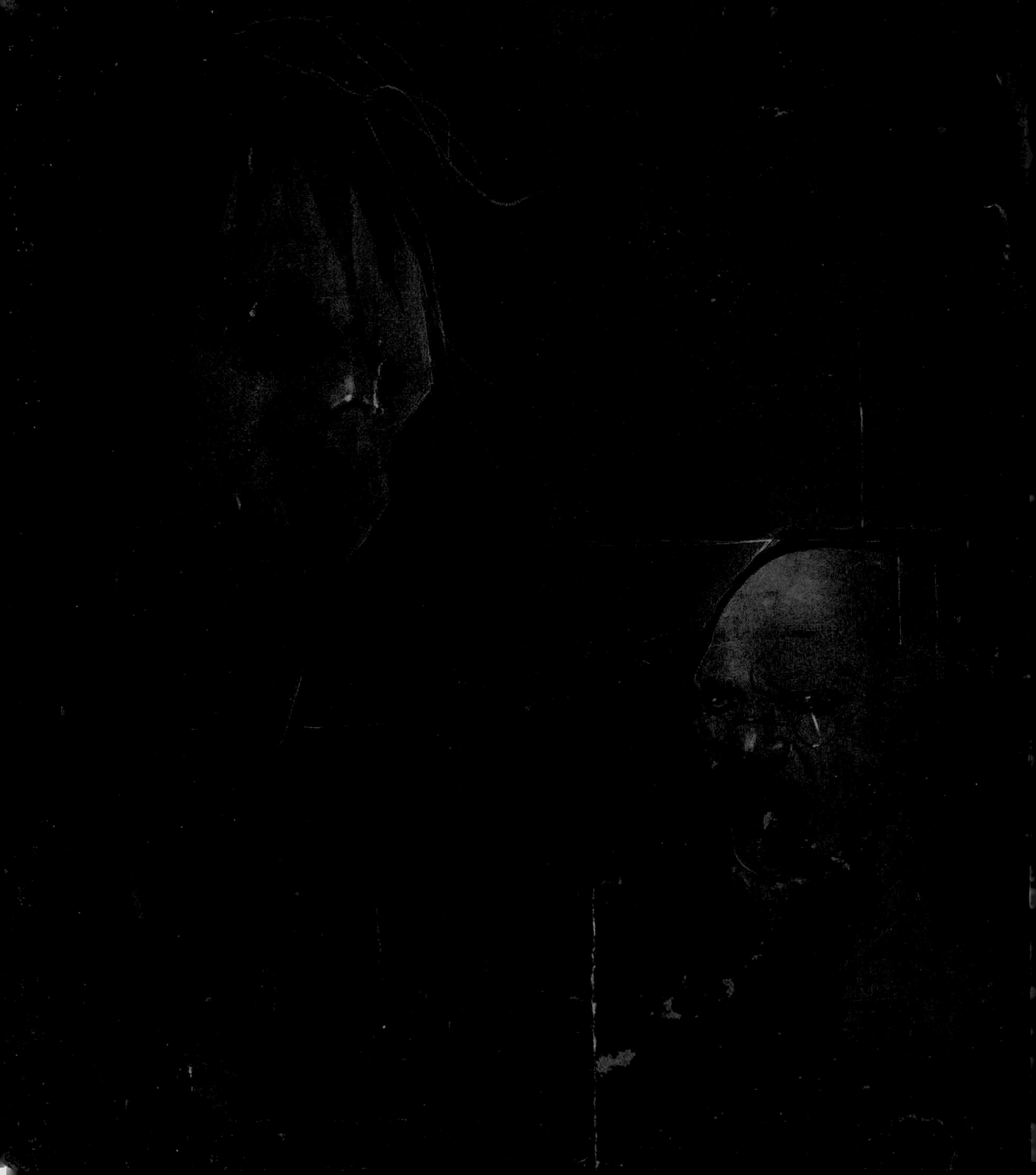